Pantheons of Isthmus

By

Oliver Allen

2021

Poems

Pantheons of Isthmus

For those who bridge ideas...

I.
Together, we are bound
Tight-lipped, credo sung
Marching in stride under the sweltering sun.

In the West Nile of Egypt
Beside the Danube River
We break for rest, as our lives have begun.

Together, the cross we bear
Has no resemblance to the moon
But instead, ideas which are now frivolously dead.

The Pharoah's tomb has room
For the lacunae of the day
But for us, the sacrifice is in our bloody heads.

Together, we are bound
Tight-lipped, credo sung
Sleeping with our books, under the goddess of moonlight.

As Egyptian larks fly by
And the buildings open up
To catch men working up a storm in the night.

We do our best with each turn
Bridging ideas like artifacts
But for us, the sacrifice is in our tempermental lives.

We are the Pantheons of Isthmus
Working class by day, Gods at night
Because we are at ease at home, when we sit down to write.

We are the Pantheons of Isthmus
Working class by day, Gods at night
Because we are able to educate ourselves, as well as our wives.

II.
Our Masters do not approve
That we decipher hieroglyphics
To try and become wiser than the rest of them too.

Archeologists and Gold Diggers
Appreciate us, and what we do
Because they can ask us anything to show them through.

But we are a chosen few
That do not get paid to peruse
Scrolls and ancient treasures beyond compare in our time.

The world knows we do not exist
Except inbetween the shadows
Of a King's tomb and a forbidden city under a thousand skies.

III.
Together, we are bound
Tight-lipped, credo sung
Marching in stride under the sweltering sun.

In the West Nile of Egypt
Beside the Danube River
We break for rest, as our lives have begun.

Together, the cross we bear
Has no resemblance to the moon
But instead, ideas which are now frivolously dead.

The Pharoah's tomb has room
For the lacunae of the day
But for us, the sacrifice is in our bloody heads.

Together, we are bound
Tight-lipped, credo sung
Sleeping with our books, under the goddess of moonlight.

As Egyptian mules pass by
And the buildings open up
To catch men and women reading in the night.

We do our best with each turn
Bridging ideas like artifacts
But for us, the sacrifice is in our tempermental lives.

We are the Pantheons of Isthmus
Working class by day, Gods at night
Because we are at ease at home, when we sit down to write.

We are the Pantheons of Isthmus
Working class by day, Gods at night
Because we are able to educate ourselves, as well as our wives.

IV.
We are the Pantheons of Isthmus
Working class by day, Gods at night

We do our best with each turn
Bridging ideas like artifacts...

We are the Pantheons of Isthmus
Working class by day, Gods at night

We do our best with each turn
Bridging ideas like artifacts...

We are the Pantheons of Isthmus
Working class by day, Gods at night
Because we are at ease at home, when we sit down to write.

We are the Pantheons of Isthmus
Working class by day, Gods at night
Because we are able to educate ourselves, as well as our wives.

But for us, the sacrifice is in our tempermental lives.
But for us, the sacrifice is in our tempermental lives.
But for us, the sacrifice is in our tempermental lives.

O.A.

The Glass Trophy Case

Rubato

Inside my Father's trophy case
There are medals, awards and trophies
From all the ceremonies he has been
But inside this glass trophy case
Is where my heart lives
Is where my heart bleeds for him
Because he only sees me when I win
When I fuckin' win.
Otherwise I am nothing to him
Just another notch on his wall
Just an Invisible Neanderthal
Incapable of other things as love
Incapable of greater things as such.

Inside my Father's trophy case
There are medals, awards and trophies
From all the ceremonies he has been
But inside this glass trophy case
Is where my heart lives
Is where my heart bleeds for him
Because he only sees me when I win
When I fuckin' win.

I'm living in a glass cage
Living on an award stage
In my Father's trophy case
But how I would love to see his face
If I smashed my way out of his trophy case...

He takes me out, when he wants to brag
To his friends at the golf course or office
And it's all worth it if I am pompous
But I don't want to be his accomplice
I want him to see me NOT as an award –
But as his son... His own flesh and blood...
The formidable one.

Vancouver, If You Leave Me

My city that I grew up in
Is changing, in ways
I can only imagine
The streets I used to know
These places are new roads
Leading me to new unknowns
Leading me down alone
To new destinations to behold

So, Vancouver, if you leave me
In the house I grew up in
And have to move on
Constructing new towns
Constructing new homes
Changing your landscape
I will wait for you
In a way,
That allows me to change
Too.

So, Vancouver, if you leave me
In the house I grew up in
And have to move on
Constructing new towns
Constructing new homes
Changing your landscape
I will wait for you
In a way,
That allows me to change
Too.

Vancouver, if you leave me
I will have my heart grieve
Like an old friend leaving me
Too.

O.A.

The Heart of a Champion

It beats, ba-doom, ba-doom
Like a steel drum in a room
Surrounded by an audience
Of blood vessels, and jewels
Like a V8 engine, Vrrrooom
Powered by high octane fuel
Calibrated by a golden rule
To never give up on anything
Like defeat or Death so soon
To win is a must for those few
Who choose, to never give up
Or unfortunately in the end, LOSE.

The Heart of a Champion
Will never concede unless
It is made to...
This is the golden rule
Of someone...
Who has a steel drum
Where their passion rules...

It beats, ba-doom, ba-doom
Like a steel drum in a room
Waiting to win again 'n again
Like a King with sweet tooth
No humble pie
Unless the Heart dies too...
To lose one cannot for the few
Who choose, to never give up
Might fortunately in the end,
As expected, with a steel heart, WIN.

O.A.

Reminiscent of You

She reminds me of you
As a warm summer's day
As a cool glass of water
As a tame autumn breeze
Blowing throughout the trees
She reminds me of you
Especially when she teases me
Especially when she breaths
Especially when she needs me
To keep her warm throughout the night
But she is nothing like you
When I see her in the morning
And I'm sharing a cup of hot cocoa
And I'm wondering why and oh no
She decides she has to go home
And then I realize, inside as I am alone
No one can replace you
No one can erase you from my memory
And now I'll have to start again a new story
Because you're in every line
You're the one behind my smile
And I know I can't hide it
I can't hide
Anywhere on this page
She reminds me of you
But the truth is, simply
There's only one person
That can make me feel
Like you do
And that's you
Yes, she reminds me
She reminds me of you
But the truth, the truth
There's only one person
In this room.
There's only one person
In this tomb.
Do I remind you
Of him too?
Or am I like you?

Confused?
The heart flutters
In its cage
Restless
On this page
One day
Clarity will sway
The pendelum my way
But until then
As the sun rises again
The morning turns
Into another day again
She reminds me of you
She reminds me of you
She reminds me of you
But the truth really is:
We're not lovers...
We're just friends.
We're just friends.

O.A.

Like an Insect to a Flame

A centipede, or moth
Ready to be devoured
By a wavering flame
Of inacted desire
Is a cruxcifiction
Of immense will
And concentration
That might not irradicate
The ugly part of who
You are like a sacrificial lamb
Might, if you follow a JUDICIAL STAR.

But then again,
Who knows who or what you really are:
As the propensity of the flame, rises...
As the propensity of the flame, rises...
As the propensity of the flame, rises...

O.A.

A Moonlight Serenade

Andante

As the pipe organ player plays
Prominently in the background,
And the quartet plucks pizzacato
Under the porcelain moonlit stars:
On the stage we both occupy,
On the terrace overlooking the pond,
Around the pillars of the palace
Priced well above and beyond
Our love; people peruse politely
Looking for a picture perfect portrait
Peformance of our polished
Demeanor and picturesque-like
Poses in capturing the hearts
Of all people involved in our
Light-hearted marriage proposal.
A fairytale of no particular place
As I pine over you pathetically
After the important persons
Dinner pontification
Of divine interrogation.

O.A.

A New Wonderful Year

If the previous year
Brought you to tears
And you're looking forward
To celebrating the New Year:
Then be brave, bold and brilliant
In stepping over the threshold
Of a tipping point in being resilient
And leaving the bad times bashfully behind
And creating a new head space in your mind.

It's a new wonderful year!!!
Time to celebrate with cheers
Time to honour those resolutions
And offer up creative lasting solutions
To get you through those tough moments
That will inevitably try and thwart your tears
You have to be brave, bold and brilliant from here
Looking forward with more than 2020 vision to be clear
Looking forward to a new year and eradicating those past fears.

It's a new wonderful year!!!
Time to celebrate with cheers
Time to honour those resolutions
Because it's a brand new start for you here...
Because it's a brand new start for you here...
Because it's a brand new start for you here...
Time to be brave, bold and brilliant to be clear.

O.A.

Ascension II

Allegro

As I float above the ground
Heading for Cloud 9
As a cherubim to the skytown
Of love, laughter and life
I am elated about the future
I am a saucer flying
I am a scarlet email
Travelling at the speed of light
Through the optik fiber at night
Tied around the cities aurora
Tied to the flamboyant sound
Tally up the toll of a cold drink
Of a life not being tied down
Of a life not being tied down
But of thirst being quenched
But to be clear, it's only for now
But to be clear, it's only for now
          Responsibility is everywhere.

My ascension into tomorrow
An intervention from sorrow
As I manipulate my senses
Into giving me more time
Into giving me more time
To fly onward up to Cloud 9
Leading me to believe love is blind
Leading me to believe love is blind
As I manipulate my senses
Into giving me more time
Into giving me more time
To fly onward up to Cloud 9
Where I will sit and read in the light
Where I will sit and read in the light
And take in the Earthly Heavenly sights...
          Goodbye yesterday, hello tonight.
          I am elated about the future of life.

Fruition

Adagio

If you have a new year's resolution
Or a wonderful new sought vision
Show your colours, your solution
Is just an idea away
Is just an idea away

Make your dreams come into fruition
By commiting to the best resolution
Of following through, the light is there
Waiting for you
Waiting for you

At the end of the tunnel
At the end of the tunnel

Love can move mountains
Love can help find your way
With motivation
Back to your commitment
After all the parties and celebrations
On that embellished new year's day
On that new start to the year of change
The light is there
Waiting for you
Waiting for you

At the end of the tunnel
At the end of the tunnel

The light is there
Waiting for you
Waiting for you

At the end of the tunnel
At the end of the tunnel

O.A.

Truth-in-Art

Art imitates life
Life imitates art
It's hard to tell
Where the truth
        Starts...

Lines upon lines
Words upon words
It's hard to tell
Where the truth
        Hurts...

Life imitates art
Art imitates life
It's hard to tell
Where the truth
        Lies...

Words upon words
Lines upon lines
It's hard to tell
Where the truth
        Hides...

Each and every
Each and every
Each and every
Each and every
        Time.

O.A.

Nocturnal Anthem

In the night as everyone sleeps
I awake to write my poetry
Or my musical score of sheets
Little do I know that I keep
Sleep-walking in my sleep
Sleep-writing as if something
Posessed me, obsessed me...

This is my Nocturnal Anthem
This is my Overture
This is my Intellectual Handle
These are my Words

Burning the midnight oil
If never a safe way to toil
But my heart and mind
Will not sleep in the nights
So I write, anything in my mind
From what I gather in daylight
The artistic experience of life...

This is my Nocturnal Anthem
This is my Overture
This is my Intellectual Handle
These are my Words

In the night as everyone sleeps
I awake to write my poetry
Or my musical score of sheets
Little do I know that I keep
Sleep-walking in my sleep
Sleep-writing as if something
Posessed me, obsessed me...

This is my Nocturnal Anthem
This is my Overture
This is my Intellectual Handle
These are my Words

My Favorite Sir Cohen Poem

Vivace

It's easy to love what you do
It's easier to read you
But my favorite poem
That speaks truth
Of how I feel
When I think
About me
And her...
About me
And her...

Are your lovely
Words:
"My Oh My."

And how I too,
Remember,
How great
It is to be "in love."

O.A.

The Roaring 20s

Fortissimo

The economic boom in the 1920s
Across this continent and others too:
Centering around Western Culture
Centering around New Renaissance
Centering around Cultural Dynamism
Centering around Pro-Feminism
Centering around a new kind of Jazz
Centering around: the telephone, movies
The automobile, television, and radio
After the Great Depression we had
Was a way to bring normalcy back
Even paving the way for Aviation
As a new business as per media.
The *annees folles* as the decade
Was known, 'the crazy years'
Showed the resilience of humanity
Relying heavily on our Sports Stars
And our beloved Celebrities too
To lead the way into a new world
Where people cheered estatically
For their home teams as national
Pride, arose dramatically inside
Every person or child in their mind...
The Roaring 20s became a catalyst
For social and economic growth
And for most it was a time of hope...
And for most it was a time of hope...
And to be honest here in 2021
It would be a blessing again, if it begun...
It would be a blessing again, if it begun...
And it helped everyone
Out of *The Great Reset* of 2020
And it helped everyone
Come *ROARING* into 2021 and beyond
And a new era had begun...

O.A.

"To who wants it"

To the happy genius of (his) household
To lo and behold the manuscript
You first published as *Al Que Quiero!*
Is an honour beyond compare
But O how I wish I had the guts
As your publisher and you made up
To offer a work that was
Part Manifesto, part Anti-blurb
O how in contempt your contemporaries
Must have felt at your chosen words
To capture the Imagism
And divine simplicity and beauty
Of both Heaven and Earth
In such poems
As: *The Artist*
And *To a Man Dying on His Feet.*

W.C.W.
Your genius daunts me.

O.A.

In a World of Automation

To withdraw some cookies
Or some Yakiudon noodles
From a vending machine
Is just the start to the day
Of automated, machined dreams.

In a world of automation:
A car window, sliding itself up or down
A driverless bus, going around and around
A taxi driverless, Uber-like car
A bank that has no tellers anymore
A mall with robots retailing stores
A grocery store that has self- checkouts
Is what a world of automation is about.

In a world of automation,
There is no room for philosophers
There is no room for poets
There is no room for sociologists
Unless they adhere to writing technicalities
About vending machines not operating well.

In a world of automation,
Everyone participates, no one is left behind
If there is a camera that follows you
Throw up an engimatic "Peace" sign!
Unless you feel, being off the grid
Is about sitting by yourself all of the time.

In a world of automation,
There is only room for ascension
There is only room for elevation
There is only room for suspension
Unless one thinks that everything won't run
Smoothly for most of the automated day.

To sit in a corner, and watch the world
To sit in a corner, and comment on things learned
To sit in a corner, and watch the clouds
To sit in a corner, and comment on things outloud

Will be a thing of the past soon.

For we philosophers, poets and sociologists
Like the psychologists and shrinks of the day
Will be too busy writing technicalities
About automated, machined dreams:
Speaking truths.

O.A.

Virgin Eyes

When I stare into the mirror
And wonder how I am tonight
Thinking of the few
Women and men
I've run away from in my life
I wonder who is this man
Afraid to hold another's hand?
Being masculine to me
Means more than being free
It means recognizing people
Who like me are afraid of intimacy
Who do not like to share a bubble
Who run away from the first signs
Of double trouble...

Some would even say,
Yes, I have "Virgin Eyes"
Because I won't let
Anyone near me soon
In my quite quiet life...
Call me "frigid"
Call me "old..."
But these days, honestly
I'd rather be left alone.

O.A.

To Kill An Albatross

To kill an Albatross
Or to kill a Dodo Bird
Takes patience, guts and time.
As this bird is rare
The air it occupies
Is reminiscent of an enigmatic sign;
And it has ways
Of coming back to life
In a simple Rime
Or other literature
Of the day and times.
But to kill an Albatross
All one has to do
Is shoot it in the heart
With an arrow or golden bullet
In which it will then significantly fall apart.
Then it is ripe for the stuffing and dinner
To feast on its scrumptious parts.

O' to kill an Albatross
Is an adventure of a lifetime
But if you already did not know
From the legend be known
There will be a price! A cost...

O.A.

Mnemonics

An apple is for knowledge
A bannana is for potassium
As an orange is for vitamin C
A kiwi is for goodness I like to eat
And a pear is for fiber, the body needs
As a plum is for sweetness, yum yum
And a chocolate strawberry is for love;
May all your dreams come into fruition
From eating the right seeds from above.

L.O.V.E.

And a chocolate strawberry is for love.
And a chocolate strawberry is for love.
And a chocolate strawberry is for love.
And a chocolate strawberry is for love.

O.A.

To She Who Matters Most

Godiva,
Goddess of the Sun, Moon, and Stars
Goodevening as you toil about your astrological duties
Goodnight as you perform your most high rituals
Goodmorning as you work through ecclestiastic routines
Goodday my King and Queen as you go about your ways

To She Who Matters Most
To She Who Made This Universe
To She Who Governs With Comforting Words
To She Who is The Ultimate Gracious Good Host
To She Who Leaves Me Alone To Write From Home

To She Who Lives On High
To She Who Gives Us All Life
To She Who Bestows Confidence
To She Who Grows As We Grow Defiant
To She Who Understands The Human Decadence...

Thank you.

O.A.

To Maya: my 1st dog

Dear bullseye of my heart
Apple of my affection
Queen of my soul
Sorry I had to go

O how I miss our walks
Through the park
And to the store
After dark

But my favorite thing
Was hearing you sing
With myself
I'll never forget
You, as long
As I live

A dog's life must be hard
Not understanding
Where love ends
And love starts

But you must know this
I'll never forget you
Your little spirit too
You'll always be
Missed...

You'll always be
Missed...

O.A.

Step into a World I Created

Largo

If Hitler was accepted as an Artist
The world we know would be different
The prospect of being loved, accepted
Can directly affect the outcome of life
And our Artistic experiences...

– The world is this poem

A shanty kind of weird world
Where love governs all possibilities
Where the Sandman brings you a Dream
A Beautiful Dream
Between the conceit & notion...
There is a sullen infested ocean of love
That carries creatures of crustacean
Into the deepest depths of desolution
I only care about a positive solution
I only care about a creative rumination
I only care as I dare to go about my life
My life, as selfish as this sounds.

– The world is this poem
              My mantra.

Step into a World I Created
Step out onto the sidewalk
Step into the light of tik tok
Step out onto the beanstalk
              And climb, climb, climb.

– This world is this poem
              Fragmented, and left behind.

The Author Inside My Head
              My Mind.

O.A.

The Brilliance of the Beguiled

The Lord is simple
The Devil is complex
They will tempt you
With money and sex.
If you give in to them
How easily you forget
They will trick you well
Promising you heaven
While you occupy hell.
Down by the street lights
They wait each dark night
For someone like you right
To come along in plain sight
And ask for directions now
And ask for salutations now
And ask for temptations now
Before leading you downtown:
To see the fiddler in the hotel
To see the boozer in the motel
To see the recluse in the lodge
Ready to play cards at all costs
And as you can see these people
Have already lost it all from the fall.

In the windowsill you stand
In the windowsill you'll understand
The Brilliance of the Beguiled
Extends far beyond Christmas time.
They will ruin your life before its time
If you give in to their way of life
If you look for a way out of yours tonight.

The Lord is simple
The Devil is complex
They will tempt you
With money and sex.
They will come around you
Looking for what they can get.

The Soundtrack of My Life

Diminuendo

As a tragic comedy goes
And as the curtain call nears
Alas, I am hearing the violins
Alas, I am hearing all the strings
Diminishing in their legato bowing
Decrescendoing in their movement
Allowing time for me to gather myself
And take a bow, like a stage actor would
At the end of a play on life and words
Before the *tutti* comes alive in the encore
Or rather *the coda* at the end of a Brahms' score.

The Soundtrack of My Life
Is a Baroque piece of me walking
Through that heavenly myriad of a door
While there is applause and laughter once more
In the amplitheater of Death as my play on life and words
Receives such mediocre reviews, and in upheaval causes an uproar:

Like a percussive stab
Or crazy cymbal crash
The big bang of it all
Will make my audience
In the end, laugh...
And someone will stand up to cheer:
"O' how this man was such a jackass!!!
Good riddance, alas, alas..."

O.A.

Psychic Jui-Jitsu

For Burroughs

I read Naked Lunch years ago
Even watched the movie
But not until I revisited
An excerpt did it have
It's full effect on me...
Years later as a man
I think I understand
How psychic jui-jitsu
Gave you the upper hand
Making you grapple
With the thoughts
Of your day.

I too use psychic jui-jitsu
To Armbar my opponents
On the blank page
Like a Behemoth in a cage
Pent up with intellectual rage.

When things get convoluted
Uprooted in the density
Of my brain, I wrestle
With words,
Verbs and adverbs
Action words,
As if I loved the herbs
Like an addictive curse...
However, my love could be worse
But I love the genius in your words:
Prose-poetics
Prose-histrionics
Prose-calastenics

I too use psychic jui-jitsu
To D'arce choke my opponents
On the blank page
Like a Mammoth in a cage
Pent up playing a chess game

I too use psychic jui-jitsu
To Mount my opponents
On the blank page
And finish the train of thought
Like a Leviathan in a cage
Pent up in a game of scholarly
                            word play.

O.A.

As Wild Rabbits Do

There is no wrong technique
To eating a carrot whole
Some like to swallow
Some like to eat it like ice cream
Some like to stuff it down
Some like to munch on it with teeth
But when you thumpty thump
The orange carrot whole
As an excited bunny knows
My face twitches as does my nose
For I am excited too
And the hair on the back of my neck
Stands up and grows
Through and through
This hare is grateful
For a snowbunny
For a summerbunny
For a playboybunny
Like you.
Like you.
Like you.

O.A.

I Want a Literary Woman

I want a Literary Woman
A Woman who likes to read
A Woman who can write poetry
I want a woman who is well-read
I want a woman who is well-kept
A woman who refuses to beg
For the finer things in life
But who will go get them
For both her and me, if I can't write
A good story or two
Basically someone who
Will support the Author in me
And support the Author in her
If she decides to write or even bother
Doing anything with literature...

I want a Literary Woman
A Woman who likes to read
A Woman who can write poetry
A Woman who has read Pendennis
The longest novel in history
A Woman who loves Lowell
A Woman who loves Milton as well
A Woman who loves Twain
A Woman who loves Musgrave
A Woman who loves T.S. Eliot
And any other Classic Authors sobeit.

I want a Literary Woman
A Woman who likes to read
A Woman who can write poetry
And does not mind if I write
And does not mind if I stay up all night
To burn the midnight lamp
If you know a woman as such
Let me know so I can get in touch
And show this Woman, my better half
And show this Woman, who I am
As a literary man, a man of songs 'n books

I want a Literary Woman
A Woman who likes to read
A Woman who can write poetry
And does not like me for my average looks
But because I love listening to good music
And because I love reading 'n writing books
And because I want to become a better cook.
These are the things for which I wish
If I can't have my ex-wife back who I miss...
These are the things for which I wish.

O.A.

The Cinematic Portrayal in My Mind

Like John Wayne at the end of a western movie
Like Jackie Chan at the end of an eastern movie
I rescue you from yourself from the barbaric institution
Of pondering, musty Death as pensive I wait for you
In the last scene with my last breath
Before, as a heroine your character fades to black
And the audience forgets to clap, clap, clap
Because they are stunned
That you aren't coming back
But instead you are dead --
I must rescue you, from
All of that...
All of that...

As Batman reigns in Gotham City
As Superman comes from Smallville
The thrill of the cinematic portrayal
Of me playing a hero in my mind
At the end of a movie
Excites me, fashionably
But I'll leave it to the men
Who train for such things
And be on my merry way
And hope you're ok
Hope you're ok
As I go home
To sit inside
To play another
Movie in my mind
To play another
Movie in my mind

And hope you'll forgive me
For forlorning you this time.
I had my memory on pause
I had my heart on rewind.
Another day, another time
I'll rescue you from my mind.

Love You Like a Violin

I'll play a symphonic rapture
On a golden violin
To enthrall your heart and capture
The essence of things
To make your heart sing
Like a caterpillar, metamorphosing
Into a multi-coloured butterfly
I'll love you like a violin
A golden violin
A Stradivarius
As a man should
Who loves music
Who loves music
Who loves music.

I'll love you like a violin
A golden violin
A Stradivarius
As a man should
Who loves music
Who loves music
Who loves music.

O.A.

To Sir Irving Layton

I read "The Cockroach"
And it had a profound effect on me
Mainly, because I have been Cupid
Or a Cockroach in my own life
Bringing people, together
Or tearing them apart
Over trivial things
As how to ingest
My insect organs
Soft-shell exterior
Or look in the mirror...
To ingest my insides
Has brought people
To advocate for me
And the Madagascar
Place I come from see...
However, I am only a cockroach
To those who know me inevitably
As a pain in the ass unfortunately...
So to you Sir Irving Layton, thank you
For writing this touching poetic story
About how love can be found anywhere
In the ugliest places even in someone like me...
Even in a "Cockroach" like me...
Poetically speaking.

O.A.

Unification of All Nations

With Love.

One love
One hand
One common goal
Together we stand
United on all fronts
Against those who demand
We do not go gentle into the light
We do not go gentle into the night
There has been too much bloodshed
There has been too much turmoil
The Earth is still our home with it's soil
The meek shall not inherit the Earth just yet
There's so much work to be done so let's not forget
To unify, all nations under the God-overlooking skies
To unify, the world with globalized economies in time
To unify, the Earth in enviromental issues to preserve life
There is still so much work to be done, before we have won.

The path of existence is not an easy one
The road to empathy can easily come undone
But I have faith in our systems in place and everyone
To help make a brighter day under a sweltering, faulty sun
To help make our streets safe again for anyone, everyone
The human spirit is a brave, fighting, undeniable force
The human condition is still a mighty science of choice
We can turn the darkest days into the brightest ones
We put a man and woman in space, and got it done
We made skyscrapers appear out of thin air, everywhere
We repaired the Ozone layer when it was breaking up there.

If we can mend the world with a heavy hand and with love
Then we can expect a better place to live for everyone
I have faith in our world leaders that they will get it done
I have faith in our world coming together as one.

I have faith in our world leaders that they will get it done
I have faith in our world coming together as one.

I have faith in our world leaders that they will get it done
I have faith in our world coming together as one.

I still believe in love
I still believe in love
I still believe in
I still believe
I still
Love.

O.A.

Fruition

Adagio

If you have a new year's resolution
Or a wonderful new sought vision
Show your colours, your solution
Is just an idea away
Is just an idea away

Make your dreams come into fruition
By commiting to the best resolution
Of following through, the light is there
Waiting for you
Waiting for you

At the end of the tunnel
At the end of the tunnel

Love can move mountains
Love can help find your way
With motivation
Back to your commitment
After all the parties and celebrations
On that embellished new year's day
On that new start to the year of change
The light is there
Waiting for you
Waiting for you

At the end of the tunnel
At the end of the tunnel

The light is there
Waiting for you
Waiting for you

At the end of the tunnel
At the end of the tunnel

O.A.

Lazarus Infection

Troubadors & Saints
Know not to wait
For the man
Sitting outside
The steel gates
Of a wealthy
Man's home;
For he waits
All alone
In sympathy
Infected
To the bones
By the immortal
Prospect
Of being left
Out in the cold
Or not being invited
Into the rich man's home.
Into the rich man's home.
Upon being risen
From the Death
Of dying as a Leopard
Or Covid-19 there
All alone on the floor...
Outside the front door...
His placard reads:
"Does not anyone care
These days, anymore?"

O.A.

Shadow Dancer

In my mind,
I dance gracefully
Like Gene Kelly
I dance passionately
Like Fred Astaire
I dance like no one
Is watching me here

I am a Shadow Dancer
In my heart I know
I have two left feet
But I love pulsating rhythms
I love to move to the beat
In my mind,
I live on Broadway
Dancing up a storm in the streets.

In my mind,
I dance wonderfully
Like Michael Jackson
I dance enthusiastically
Like Gregory Hines
I dance like no one
Is watching my big lie

I am a Shadow Dancer
In my heart I know
I have two left feet
But I love pulsating rhythms
I love to move to the beat
In my mind,
I live on Broadway
Dancing up a storm in the streets.

And if you give me a partner
Let her be as bold as me!!!
Let her have two right feet
So we can move to Broadway
And dance up a storm in the streets.

I am a Shadow Dancer
In my heart I know
I have two left feet

I am a Shadow Dancer
In my heart I know
I have two left feet

But in my mind,
I live on Broadway
Dancing up a storm in the streets.

O.A.

Sky Castle of Heaven

Sunlight, piercing
The thin vale of a window pane
Crossed with an armoury of bars
As angels with halos just guard
The almighty home of God on high.

This sky castle...
This heaven flowing all around
Reflects the most ethereal light
Through pillars of unwavering air...
Through pillars of unwavering air...

This sky castle...
Has many who have not dreamed
About the creatures who come
Riding the rainfall day after day
When the angels cry their tears.

This sky castle...
Is for any amount of growing fears
That this castle on a cloud, skytown
Does not house a most loving God
Does not house a most loving One.

This sky castle...
This heaven flowing all around
Reflects the most ethereal light
Through pillars of unwavering air...
Through pillars of unwavering air...

O.A.

Grateful

How many times can I give thanks
And praise?
To you my Lord for blessing me
With insurmountable ways?
I am grateful to be alive
I am grateful dearly inside
I am grateful for a chance at life
These things I do not take lightly
Like a new lease on an automobile
I am driving into tomorrow full steam ahead
I am running ahead of the pack in my dreams
I am swimming in a wide ocean of anomousity
And surviving with the sharks and octopuss of the day
As a creature who does not give up in any possible way.

How many times can I give thanks
And praise?
To you my Lord for blessing me
With insurmountable ways?
I am grateful to be alive
I am grateful dearly inside
I am grateful for a chance at life
I am grateful to have you as my guide
I am grateful to have you on my side
Through the thick and thin of it all, afterall
You know best for me and my family
You know the best situations for me
And I am grateful to have you as my compass
I am grateful more than you will ever know...

How many times can I give thanks
And praise?
To you my Lord for blessing me
With insurmountable ways?

O.A.

Masterclass of Inebriates

Adagio

Stuck in an elevator with you
With no place to go or turn to
I ask you to tell me some stories
About your early days of glory

In a masterclass of inebriates
I am a student to your teachings
I am high and drunk on the life
You present to me in your stories
In a masterclass of inebriates
I only ask that you pass the whiskey
And that you do not bore me
That you do not bore me

Stuck in an elevator with you
With no place to go or turn to
I ask you to tell me some stories
About your early days of glory

In a masterclass of inebriates
I am a student to your teachings
I am high and drunk on the life
You present to me in your stories
In a masterclass of inebriates
I only ask that you pass the whiskey
And that you do not bore me
That you do not bore me

O.A.

Diabolical Disdain

If you hate someone or something
To the point you start to fabricate stories
About that someone or something
You might start to hate yourself just the same.
You might start to hate yourself just the same.

Diabolical disdain
For a competitive point of gain
For fame can mess up your name
See karma can mess up your game
Make you start from the beginning again.
Make you start from the beginning again.
So it's best to just turn the page...
Or just walk the other way.

O.A.

Appropriation of the Tomahawk Kid

By

Oliver Allen

A Dedication to the Beats Generation

Appropriation of the Tomahawk Kid

As legend has it, not all poets in San Fransico
Were a part of the Beat Generation, some poets
Became the catalyst behind the Beat Generation...

"Is that him? Is that Allen?" I asked, lighting up a cigarette...
"Do we have him under surveillance?" I continued...
"And what about the other two?"

"Yes, we do" replied my partner Garrett,
Downing some port wine brought to our table
By our ditsy waitress.

"What about the other two? Who are they?"
"Jack Kerouac and William Burroughs,
One's a homojunkie and the other's a schizoid..."

"Schizophrenic?" I asked, laughing under my breath.
"Does he talk to himself? Or at least answer his own questions?"

"Fuckin' spouts rhetoric fit for an insane asylum!!!
And the other's a lover of another..."

"Easy," I said pushing the bottle of port wine,
Closer to my partner Garrett...

"Why are these guys under surveillance, anyways?..."
I asked leaning back in my chair...

The event in which we were situated, was getting fuller
By the second. They had closed down the night club
In which we were sitting, to allow some avante-garde
Poets to read their hot shit tonight...

This happened frequently, in this downtown area
Of San Francisco, we were haunting...
At the *Pur Loins* night club, all the Artists, Bohemians,
Pedalers, and Literary Junkies gathered on Friday nights
To hear some DeadBeat Loser lose his or her mind
On stage at this Go-Go club...

Tonight, here at the *Pur Loins* the feature loser I found out
Was a cowboy hat wearing Native American Indian
Calling himself the Tomahawk Kid...

"Federal Bureau of Investigations wants to know what these guys
Are doing even before they do it..." Garrett calmly replied,
Downing some more of his port wine, looking right at me.

"Wow," I answered back, crossing my arms, "these guys made
Our naughty list, nice!!!"

"This guy Allen Ginsberg is working on some obscene material
That is derogatory, and offensive...
He's the head of the pack, the other two are his right and left men
But there's a shitshow cast of characters around them at all times.
This one DeadBeat Loser named: Ferlinghetti runs a publishing house
Called "City Lights," a paperback publishing model, fashioned
After those publishing houses in Paris, I heard; situated downtown
San Francisco Bay area..."

"Near Alcatraz?" I asked curiously...
"One trolley ride away..." commented my FBI partner Garrett.

The audience were a group of misfits in their late 20's to mid 30's
As aforementioned, the Bohemian class of the late 1950's
Artistic district of San Francisco.
The smell of hashish mixed with tobacco smoke could be smelt
In the air around us...

I tried to cover my nose with the sleeve of my jacket,
As I did not want to come home to my new wife
Smelling of a hemp factory, and sprayed a couple squirts
Of cologne all around us...

As I sat there in disgust at the sexual antics of the night
On display before my eyes, I watched the odd trio
Of night marauders: Ginsberg, Kerouac, and this fellow Burroughs
Continually throw their hands up, pass cigarettes around them
And wondered if they knew or cared that they attracted
The attention of the FBI...

By the time the Tomahawk show was about to commence,
I could hear Ginsberg chanting a monotonous array
Of jibberish quite loud that sounded like he was yelling:
Moloch! Moloch! Nightmare of Moloch! Moloch the loveless!
Mental Moloch! Moloch the heavy judger of men!

"What is he doing, the show is about to start!!!"
Exclaimed Garrett who was also watching Ginsberg
Make a fool of himself, yelling with his hands in the air...

"I don't know, but I'll snap some pictures for our files,"
I suggested inching closer with my polaroid camera.

As I snapped a few headshots, the lights around us dimmed
And the sound of native drums, and native chants
Could be heard throughout the *Pur Loins*, night club.

"Introducing, the one and only Indian Cowboy from the West,
Who'll read you a tantalizing poem or two, steal your heart,
Your money, and then make off with the loot; the man,
The myth, the legend... The one and only... Tomahawk Kid!!!"

The crowd, cheered and clapped out of disillusionment,
And perhaps out of utter chaos and calamity...
The decibel level in *Pur Loins* was electric and deafening...

Garrett and I stood up to get a better view,
Of the DeadBeat Poets, and this Tomahawk Kid character.
Now San Francisco had alot of strange, and wacky people
But this man on stage dressed in a shawl of feathers,
Bison-skin boots, beating a drum with his left hand,
While weilding a Tomahawk in his right hand,
Took the cake!!!

I thought to myself, his only occupation must be
A Bohemian Indian, carrying on like this...
He came out on stage throbbing his body back and forth
Convulsing heroically, passionately, beating his drum,
Tied to his waist, and chanting: "Way-Na-Na-Na
Way-Na-Na-Na..." melodically.

Once he centered himself on stage, he motioned
For everyone to be quiet...
In silence he pulled a notebook, from his back pocket
And began reciting some poetry lines that made it intense,
The atmosphere...

"This is from a poetry collection entitled:"

"Give Me Back My Land, Mr. White Man..."

I immediately looked over at Ginsberg for a reaction,
And he began to *Howl* extremely loud, egging
The Tomahawk Kid onward...

        "This Land Belongs to the Free...

        This land belongs to the free
        Belongs to my ancestry
        Belongs to both you and me
        Belongs to all my family

        You took it away
        The day Christopher Columbus
        Sailed into our bay
        You wrestled it from our arms
        Imposed taxes
        And overtook our farms

        The world was not flat
        A piece of land to fall off
        This is not a racist attack
        But a plea to ask you to stop
        Stop killing us
        Stop killing us
        Treaties need us
        Treaties need us

        This land belongs to the free
        Belongs to my ancestry
        Belongs to both you and me
        Belongs to all my family

This land belongs to the free
If you imprison me
If you kill me
Every face like me
Animals of the land will revolt
Mother Nature will advocate for our humanity
Mother Nature will advocate for our humanity
Mother Nature will advocate for our humanity..."

Folks started to clap uncontrollably, while the Tomahawk Kid took a bow...
He immediately rode the wave of emotion, and recited another powerful piece...

"Transcendental

Imagine a world without pain
A world for nothing to gain
A transcendental world
Between time and space
And the only way to live
In this realm
Was to balance the scales
On a metaphysical pendelum.
The only way to live
Was to allow for more freedom
Was to allow for more freedom
Between folks and their friends
In this transcendental, magical,
Exceptional, prolific, conceptual,
Intercontinental, transcendental
Realm...

Imagine this world
And you will begin
To understand
Heaven..."

The crowd was fired up! Even more now, so the Tomahawk Kid decided
To read a familar but older poem, that was not his,
But from the reknowned poet William Blake...
Who struck Ginsberg as being incredulous.

He started by offering a disclaimer on his next poem: "although this poem
Is not mine, it still shines, and is from a more fruitful mind
Of the Romantic Period
Poet William Blake..."

"The Sick Rose

O Rose, thou art sick!
The invisible worm,
That flies in the night,
In the howling storm,

Has found out thy bed
Of crimson joy;
And his dark secret love
Does thy life destroy..."

Suddenly, there was a noise in the crowd, as the Tomahawk Kid
Finished reading this poem...
I looked over to where the noise was coming from
And it was Allen shouting, ranting and raving wildly in the audience.
He was chanting aloud:

Moloch! Moloch! Nightmare of Moloch! Moloch the loveless!
Mental Moloch! Moloch the heavy judger of men!
Moloch! Moloch! Nightmare of Moloch! Moloch the loveless!
Mental Moloch! Moloch the heavy judger of men!

I didn't see it coming right away, but Burroughs sure did...
A wild fan hurled a beer bottle in their direction
And just in time, Kerouac and Burroughs ducked
While, the bottle smashed Allen right in his face!!!
"SHUT THE HELL UPPP!!!" A large man belted,
Staring vehemently at the 3 men...

"Should we help them out???" I asked my partner Garrett.
"Hold on, let's see how they handle this situation..."

But it was too late. Burroughs took to the offence,
And hurled a bottle back at the instigator...
Actually missing, but as a madman possesed

He ran over to the douchbag who threw the bottle
And punched him in the face... Kerouac jumped on his back.
And a straight out brawl ensued...
Ginsberg recovered, and grabbed a wooden folding chair
And ran over and smashed it on the back of Kerouac
By mistake... However, as everyone was now
Scrambling to leave, or join in on the Hoopla fighting
The sound of sirens could be heard outside
Getting closer, and closer towards them...

Burroughs had the man in a headlock by now
And the large man's girlfriend, a tiny little thing
Was screaming: "Murdererrr!!! Bloody Murder!!!"
While Kerouac lay sitting on the ground,
Hunched over, doubled-over in pain...

Our ditsy waitress that served Garrett and I
Was also screaming, running around
Trying to protect her tray of beers:
"Leave them alone!!! You have to pay...
Like everyone else you Mutherfuckers!!!"

Allen Ginsberg, saw her holding the tray
Up high by his head, standing behind her
And helped himself out to a pint of draft beer
That he gulped down, as the sound of sirens
Stopped outside the Go-Go club *Pur Loins*...

"Let's get out of here!!!" Cried Kerouac
Standing back up, but it was too late...
The Fun Police had arrived to break up
The Fun...
The Fun everyone was having...

The Tomahawk Kid just stood there on stage
Dumbfounded, and in utter shock at the scene
However, he had the common sense to take the mic
And release one last piece of wisdom to the crowd...
"The Police are here!!! Runnnnnnnnnnnnnnn!!!"

Ginsberg grabbed Kerouac, and Burroughs
But an officer grabbed Ginsberg, and handcuffed him.

The 3 men were arrested, along with half a dozen others.
The Tomahawk Kid was also arrested as well
For trying to flee, as soon as the Police arrived.

I tried not to bust out laughing, while Garrett and I
Left the night club unscathed, but my partner
Made me realize that FBI surveillance
Meant that wherever the Poetic Misfits went
We were supposed to go as well too...

So Garrett did the only thing left to do
And reached out and punched the nearest officer
To us... So we got arrested too...
They threw us in the Paddywagon
With the DeadBeat Poets, the Tomahawk Kid,
The Large Man, his tiny girlfriend, and our ditsy waitress.

Downtown, San Francisco, here we come...
Downtown, San Francisco, here we come...
      In the back of the Paddywagon.
      In the back of the Paddywagon.
      The sirens blared...

...

"Why did you punch me?" The Large Man asked Burroughs.
"Are you serious, Man!!?" Asked Burroughs standing up in the drunk tank,
"You threw a bottle at us!!! And it even hit my friend in the face!!!"
Allen Ginsberg placed his left hand on his jaw, and massaged it stubbornly,
Adding insult to injury...

"Fuck dudes, I was drunk sorry..."
"Drunk!!?" Stammered Burroughs, "You ruined the show, and got us all
Arrested... And it was a great show!!!"
"Yes, it was," replied Ginsberg.
"Yes, it was," answered Kerouac, flicking his lighter.
"Sure was" chimmed in the Large Man's tiny girlfriend...
"I was making a fortune in tips!!!" Cried our ditsy waitress.
"Thank you," said the Tomahawk Kid, who had been quiet up until now...
"It was my first show here on the San Francisco circuit..."

"Where are you from, originally?" Asked Ginsberg curiously...

"South Dakota," he hesitantly replied, "Listen," he continued
"Either you're with us, or against us..."
Allen Ginsberg chose his words carefully: "I am a friend
Of the Red Movement, believe me I know what it's like
To be oppressed, being Jewish and all, so to answer
You're question right now, Yes I can dig it..."

"Well my people and tribes are working on something big..."
"Yeah like what???" Replied Burroughs, standing in front
Of Ginsberg and the Tomahawk Kid.
"You know Alcatraz?"
"Yeah," answered Ginsberg leaning in closer.
"We're going to take it over!!! In a few years, and march to Washington..."
"WHAT!!?? Far out..." Cried Kerouac.
"Yeah, man my tribe leader, and other AIM members are working on it..."
"Are you from the future, man?" Asked Ginsberg, smiling.
"Maybe," replied the Tomahawk Kid, smiling back.
"Here! Here, are some beads for good luck," he continued, pulling a string
Of beads from out his shawl pocket...

I sat there quietly, with my partner Garrett listening
To these DeadBeat Poets, converse about their conspiracies...

"How do you know, William Blake's work?" Asked Ginsberg once again.
"College in Minnesota," responded the Tomahawk Kid,
"He was on the reading list for the Romantics, man..."
"Well, he's one of my favorites... Do you feel assimilated in learning
About an English Poet like Blake in school?"

"No not at all, a poet is a poet, no matter from where,
As long as they love language and life..."
"Assimilation is everywhere now," suggested Kerouac, "it's not right."
"That's why we must stay vigilant," purported Burroughs,
Folding his fingers together...
"Stick it to the Man, however we can..."
"Man, you guys are talking like you understand,
Where I'm coming from..."

As the Tomahawk Kid was having his 3 aficionados arrive at the same
Wavelength, as himself, and he was enjoying the conversation
An officer came into the drunk tank, to speak to everyone:

"Tonight, is your lucky night, all of you in here have made bail,
Except you Large Man, and your tiny girlfriend..."

"WHATTT!!!?" Screamed the Large Man, in standing up.
"Sir back down," Chirped his tiny girlfriend
"You deserve this, we're not going anywhere...
Call your Mother!!!"

"WHOOOOOOO!!!" Yelled Burroughs, grabbing his hat.
"All of us?" Asked the Tomahawk Kid...
"Almost all of you" replied the police officer...
"Who posted our bail???" Asked Allen Ginsberg, wondering.

Just as everyone was gathering their belongings,
Lawrence Ferlinghetti could be seen, waiting in the lobby
Of the police station, pacing back and forth.

"Ferly!!! My, my, my old friend, nice to see you again," said Kerouac,
Giving the man a hug...
"What happened to you guys, I was waiting at the bookstore all night,
Until I got word, you guys had been arrested..."
"Long story chap..." Answered Burroughs.

The group of Misfit DeadBeat Poets walked into the foggy night
Of downtown San Francisco like Rockstars...
Even with our ditsy waitress by their sides, posting bail as well.
I noticed, looking through the station doors...
Champions of the Night, I thought to myself.

In the morning, Ginsberg lay half asleep, wondering if he had
Experienced a Dream Sequence, or if he had had a Premonition
Or had he really been out last night...
On his chest, he felt a paperback book of William Blake's
Complete poetic works, that he now pushed aside to the floor.

His jaw felt sore, and his mouth was extremely dry, with halitosis
On his breath.
Ginsberg wondered, as he stared into the mirror,
If he had experienced a Dream Sequence or Premonition...
Who was this Tomahawk Kid really?
Why was his appropriation needed last night?

And what was this Red Movement, he was rambling about?
These questions and more, were on Allen's mind
As he blended his morning coffee.

As he sipped his Expresso, he noticed that he was wearing
All his evening clothes still, and in his pant pockets
Were a set of beads, that he pulled out, which made him realize
Maybe it was not a Premonition afterall...
However, nonetheless he felt hungover, had a headache,
And felt like one "Sick Rose..."
Allen Ginsberg, thought to himself, *what a wild night!!!*
He looked up at the calender, and then back
Down to the string of beads in his hands...

The End

Thank you:

Ginsberg
Kerouac
Burroughs
Ferlinghetti
Tomahawk Kid

O.A.

Why I Write.

A girl broke my heart
When I was a small boy
And I had no choice
But to write it down;
My feelings,
As they came out.
As repetition speaks:
The weeks to weeks,
Became months to months,
And my vocabulary grew
As I grew into my shoes.
No longer did a woman
Command my heartless pen
But it was a catalyst for me
To write, over and over again.
The poetry I now speak,
As the moon and stars do shine;
Is from the heart, upon which is mine,
Dear mine -
But why I write -
Is simply to escape the idle thoughts,
Of my mind.

O.A.

Bleed

For those still bleeding alone...

Human desire
Is fueled by the fire
Burning as a stoked chimney
To the soul
Rising ash embers will only grow
When the fire is stoked by someone
Who understands how to poke it
Who understands how to choke it
To make a person suffocate inside
Until they burst with inevitable fire
Until they bleed with incandescent light
As the fuel for success runs through their veins
Like a runaway, runaway, enamoured freight train
Rolling through the cosmos, unapologetically untamed
Like a wild bull, or ram, on a mountainside of sugar cane
Grazing along side the burning bushes of Paradise Re'gained
Laughing at the archangel Moloch as he tempers his blade
To cut you down for not understanding the insane aptitude of fame.

Human desire
Is fueled just the same
One inch away from madness
As the miles add up in the pouring rain
You can run away, but the truth will mitigate you
Infiltrate you, investigate you, commandeer you
To see if you really want to play
To see if you really want to play
A game of Russian Roulette
To see if you really want the pain
Of the price of human desire:
The fortune
The accolades
The spotlight
The fame.

O.A.

The Heart Knows

If you're down on your luck
And frankly don't give a fuck
And feel like you're wasting time
Reciting every "thank you again..."
And aren't thinking with a clear mind
The heart knows...

If you've lost your moral compass
And can't get your life back on track
And can't get your old natural self back
Thinking you'll never be 100 percent
And feel like you're wasting time
The heart knows...

The heart knows
When the bird has flown the coup
And your mind is like Alphabet soup
Complicating the things that count
Because the heart will burst with emotion
Insurrected by the mouth
Like a volcano
Erupting from down
South.

If the world stops to let you off
And frankly you've given all you've got
And think it's time to throw in the towel
Reading things that only make sense
To you and makes you want to grovel
At anyone
Everyone
At once
The heart knows...
The heart knows...
The heart knows...

It's the mind that has to let go.

O.A.

Stay the Course

They will kill you
They have told you that
Your fears, tears and demons
But if you stay the course
Heading for a new chapter
You will make peace with the Lord.

The Captain of this ship,
Does not need a compass
North, West, East and South
Does not matter in any amount now
But to walk through the fire
To break bread with smugglers and thiefs
To drink at last call, and then bed a bar maid
To watch the sunrise, in your own eyes
To watch the seagulls soar above in peace
To near the end of a night of innocence
And claim victory in a morning of insolence
To besmirch the glory unto thy self
Only to stay the course
Heading for a natural disaster
You will make peace with the Lord.
You will inevitably die.

But that which does not kill you
Will make you stronger,
For you will die
But also reinvent yourself
Like never before.

Do not back down
Do not run and hide
Yesterday, today and tomorrow
Will all collide in due time
But to seize the moment
Like a ripple effect in the epicenter of life
Like a momentous ball of thunder
Like a day that no one ever forgets
Like a night that everyone remembers
And to spin Death on its heels, to turn it around:

For he wants you to reinvent yourself
Augment, to a higher self
In ways only a glass of water can do
When you're thirsty for a glass of bourbon too.
In reality, your life is your life
No one cares what you do or cannot do.

They will kill you
They have told you that
Your fears, tears and demons
But if you stay the course
Heading for a new chapter
You will make peace with the Lord.

If you stay the course
If you stay the course
And do not break but bend in the wind,
You will inevitably die.
You might also win
If you listen,
But also reinvent yourself
Like never before.

If you stay the course
Heading for a new chapter
You will make peace with the Lord.

O.A.

Never Go to Bed Angry

For the closest person to me.

Even if you don't agree
Never go to bed angry

Even if you're at fault
Never go to bed angry

Even if you feel good
Never go to bed angry

For you might wish you would
Have told your love enough
So he or she would have dreams
Not about your angry reddened face
But dreams about a quiet tranquility
In your place of solace in your case;
Than be rather annoyed in a soliloquy
To a nosy neighbouring audience.

Even if you don't agree
Never go to bed angry
For if God decides
The time is right
It might be the last night
You and he or she ever fight...

O.A.

We, the Majority

No man is an island
No man can do it all alone
But the power of the "We"
We, the majority
Is discernible in its resourcefulness.

We, the majority
Decide it all
We, the majority
Decide when it begins and ends
The power of the "We"
Is greater than just a "He, She, or Me"
The power of the "We"
Is incredibly noteworthy
In all salutations.

No man is an island
No man can do it all alone
But the power of the "We"
We, the majority
Is discernible in its resourcefulness.

I, the minority
Only have partiality
I, the minority
Can only agree to work with you
Its not a Black or White thing
Its a power of the "We" get it thing
The power of the "We"
Is incredibly noteworthy
In all salutations.

No man is an island
No man can do it all alone
But the power of the "We"
We, the majority
Is discernible in its resourcefulness.

O.A.

Elegance

In the midnight hour
She comes to me
In a red satin dress
Elegantly...
Elegantly, staring
Across the room
As my temptress
Wanting to seduce
My burning soul
My yearning soul.
In the midnight hour
She comes to me
In a red satin dress
Elegantly...
Elegantly, I wait
Wait for her to come
And stand next to me
Bearing her gifts
For me to open
If she too thinks I am
Of elegance...
Elegantly, I close my eyes
As she commands
As she demands
Because I am
In her world now
And she has her plan
To make me understand
She is in control
Of this scenario
Of elegance...

In the midnight hour
She comes to me
In a red satin dress
Elegantly...
And all I can do...
Is wait patiently.

Life and Death

From the girth
As a baby calf
I crawl into the dirt
As my mother gives birth
To her dreams, within me
And in this maternal sanctuary
There are my brothers and sisters
Who have all come before me to teeth.

From the shadows
As a part of Death's daily duties
I walk through an entrance like no other
I say goodbye to my family and my mother
As this is as surreal as it gets, as a matador
For my eternal performance, playing out in parts
That I have not imagined or reimagined before
All I have left to do is walk through those arena doors.

The beginning and the end
The beginning and the end
The beginning and the end
Are one, with life and death.

These are the days
Full of respect
And disrespect,
How easily one forgets
How intertwined
Is Life and Death.

I am a bull and matador
I am a life and death metaphor
I am one step away
From becoming intertwined
In a struggle of day and night
A tug-o-war of dark and light
As the piece of bull*$%! I was
Stares me now in my eyes.
I have changed.

I am now an angry matador
Who calls the big bluff
As bull
And spears my own mane
In the name
Of the crying shame, game.
I have changed.

The beginning and the end
The beginning and the end
The beginning and the end
Are one, with life and death.

These are the days
Full of respect
And disrespect,
How easily one forgets
How easily one forgets
How easily one forgets
Life can be momentous
Life can be adventurous
But Death...
But Death...
But Death...
Can end us.

O.A.

Months Left to Live

Waiting to die
Waiting to die
As I sit back and close my eyes
And think back on all my memories
The good and not so awful times.

The sun is going down
The world is going to sleep
But I lay awake in this bed
Counting bottles of gin and sheep
If only the loser in me could be beat.

The moon is coming up
The sky is a midnight green
The northern lights are bright
But my own Aurora is in my mind
If only my senses would ease up on me.

I have months left to live
I have unfinished business
With my landlord and banks
I have unfinished business
With my family and friends
I have unfinished business
With everything coming to an end.

Waiting to die
Waiting to die
As I sit back and close my eyes
And think back on all my memories
The good and not so awful times.

But O' how I wish
I could light one more cigarette
I could taste one more vinaigrette
I could drink one more glass of gin
I could gorge myself and eat a sandwich
And then tell Death to piss off again
And come back in a few years
When I have raised a glass

With a few more cheers
O' how I wish
I wish...

Waiting to die
Waiting to die
As I sit back and close my eyes
And think back on all my memories
The good and not so awful times.

Waiting to die
Waiting to die
As I sit back and close my eyes
I would cry, but then that would make you
Feel sorry for me
Benevolently
And I've lived
One hell of a life...
I've put up one
Hell of a fight.

O.A.

A Poet's Corner

In a poet's corner
I sit, pensive
Affirming quantitative
And qualitative thoughts
Of erudition.
Linguistically, I am removed
From all self-righteous notions
That a thought lives up on a cloud
But rather in the systematic root of things
The internet of things, ricocheted from the synergy
Of all nouns and pronouns interconnected
In a way where all living organisms thrive accordingly.

In a poet's corner
I sit, pensive
Sifting through words
Simplifying ideas
And looking up at the clouds
Wondering what I'll have for dinner?
Maybe I'll look on the internet
For a new recipe...

O.A.

My Starlit Heroine

It's not hard to love you
It's not hard to believe in you
Because you're perfect
Symmetrical, impeccable, flawless
Like an undiscovered gem stone
Or diamond in the rough
Because you're tough
You're one hell of a card hand
Aces high, or a royal flush
It's not hard to love you
It's not hard to believe in you
You have an audience of love
You have an audience of love.

But myself?
I'm easy to forget
I'm a piece of shit
Because I do not appreciate you
I do not see what others do
Like a selfish person who loathes
Perfection, direction, but craves attention
You're one hell of a card hand
Aces high, or a royal flush
It's not hard to love you
It's not hard to believe in you
You have an audience of love
You have an audience of love.

Except one, one thing
I will never be enough
Enough for you to love
For your audience of love
For your audience of love
And as they clap for you
They laugh at me as your stage hand
I am remissed at this unfortunate chance
You are the Starlit Heroine, and I'm just in the band
You don't need me anymore, I understand
It's not hard to love you
It's not hard to believe in you

You have an audience of love
You have an audience of love.

O.A.

Universe

Inside God's mind
Inside a garden of thoughts
Inside a plethora of ideas
Are infinite possibilities...
Of many worlds or galaxies
Beyond our realization
Or preconception.
But the sheer amazement
And wonder when I look up
Into the midnight sky
And see a constellation
Makes me ponder upon the stars.
If the universe is in God's mind
And God is omnipresent
Am I staring into the line of sight
Of one of God's billions
Of all-seeing eyes?

Inside God's mind
Inside a garden of thoughts
Inside a plethora of ideas
Are infinite possibilities...
Like a fresh crop of wheat
Waiting to be harvested
And spread out on the table of life.
The planets, moons and stars
Are the flowers blooming
With bountiful radiance
Aglow inside the universe
With the comets, asteroids
And other planetary debris
Like after thoughts
Of bulbs of plants that did not grow
Inside the garden of Eden.

Inside God's mind
Inside a garden of thoughts
Inside a plethora of ideas
Are infinite possibilities...

Churning new life beyond the cosmos
Waiting to be discovered...
Waiting to be discovered...
Waiting to be discovered...
By a human lifeform
With a kindred mindframe
For a universe
Reimagined
For a universe
Reborn.

O.A.

The Big Bad Lonesome Wolf

In the house
Where my family grew up,
There was a wolf
Living among the few of us;
And this big, bad wolf,
Lonesome recluse,
Would sometimes threaten
To blow the house down
With its angry words it choosed.
This big bad lonesome wolf
Would puff its chest up,
And howl in the middle of the night,
If my mother did not cook
Dinner the way it liked;
Or it would hurl insults
To all 3 of us: my sister, mother and I
If we did not look it in the eyes,
After a night of intoxication,
Sitting in the recliner chair at sunrise.

Oh how I wanted to grow fangs
Like the ones the big bad wolf had,
And pierce its voracious vernacular
With words that hurt even more than words!!!
But the day would come, would come
When it grew tired in its bellowing lungs,
And my own lungs would grow too,
As a pair of automatic vocabulary tools,
Allowing me to howl back at its rude
Loquacious and insatiable inept attitude.

Yes, the day would come, would come
When this big bad lonesome wolf
Would meet its match under the sun,
And my mother, sister, cousin and aunt
Would never hear it howl again as it wanted.
For the big bad lonesome wolf...
Would finally leave our house as daunted...

Purgatory

What is purgatory?
I ask myself this
Before I seal my own Death
With a supple kiss
Before I twist the blade
Between my own lips...
In a few minutes
I am sitting, naked and cold
Between Heaven and Hell
In a white space that extends
For miles and miles...

There are other people here
A woman in a coffin
A man lying in a box
A seagull which is sitting on a rock
All a part of my imagination
Before I realize I cannot talk.

What is purgatory?
I ask myself this
Is this a place where the Devil
And his archangels live?
Is this a place where God
And his Heavenly angels forgive?

I am cold and alone
Because I decided
I would rather be here
Than miserable for a short time
At my humble abode
At home.

But yet there are other people here
A woman in a coffin
A man lying in a box
A seagull which is sitting on a rock
All a part of my imagination
Before I realize I cannot talk.

All around me
All around me
Buzzing about me
Buzzing about,
Are flies, thousands.
All around me
All around me
And the messenger
Beezlebub
Is calling to me,
Intrepidly.

I am sitting, naked and cold
Between Heaven and Hell
In a white space that extends
For miles and miles...

I am cold and alone
Because I decided
I would rather be here
Than miserable for a short time
At my humble abode
At home.

But yet there are other people here
A woman in a coffin
A man lying in a box
A seagull which is sitting on a rock
All a part of my imagination
Before I realize I cannot talk.
I cannot talk.

What is purgatory?
I ask myself this
Before I seal my own Death
With a supple kiss
Before I twist the blade
Between my own lips...

O.A.

In Another Lifetime, We Could Be Friends

Comrade,
Are you not entertained?
Are you still sane?
The War is over
Why do you still want blood
To spill in our names?
The sun has gone down
The moon is rising high
The waves are crashing ashore
Why do you still want more war?
The other men have gone home
To be with their children and wives
But the look from your soul into my eyes
Tells me you're not happy with your life
The world is empty for you without strife
Some men love to fight, are you still looking
For a fight with me as we leave this battlefield
Tonight?

In another lifetime, we could be friends
In another lifetime, this could all end
In another lifetime, we could end this war
In another lifetime, we could be so much more
In another lifetime.

Hunger,
Hunger breeds deceit
But hunger for love breeds peace
If its what you dream of when you sleep
The War is over
Why is there anger you still keep?
The sun has gone down
The moon is rising high
The waves are crashing ashore
Why do you still want more war?
The other men have gone home
To be with their children and wives
But the look from your soul into my eyes
Tells me you're not happy with your life

Some men love to fight, are you still looking
For a fight with me as we leave this battlefield
Tonight?

In another lifetime, we could be friends
In another lifetime, this could all end
In another lifetime, we could end this war
In another lifetime, we could be so much more
In another lifetime.

In another lifetime
We could be friends, forevermore
We could be friends, forevermore.

O.A.

The Bartender at Tigh-Na-Mara

I've heard the best drinks in Parksville, BC
Come from a bartender or two
From the dinner service at Tigh-Na-Mara
The spa resort that I saw in a review
A place I would love to visit one day
And take my family there aswell too.
The bartender at Tigh-Na-Mara
I would ask him or her to make
Any cocktail or drink on the rocks
And then make small talk about the lot.
I would open up as anyone would
To a bartender in a remote part of the woods
About my career as a freelance writer
And ask what kind of trees are these around here?
But the best part about this scenario
If I had dinner after taking to the Grotto
Would be, asking why such a wonderful resort
Did not have reviews about their drinks as sport?

O' how I would love to visit Tigh-Na-Mara
And talk trees, spirits, and history
With a bartender or two
Or anyone who would share a story with me
While I sipped on a Mohita after the dinner menu.

O.A.

Tearful Eyes

The years gone by
Brings watershed tears
To my wild-moon eyes
As the cresent shape
Of my eyelids procreate
A dilapidated mindstate
Of yearning for another
Year or so to procrastinate
In bringing about change
To my depreciating ways.
In a wishing well of life
Around my neighbourhood
I cast a penny or two
And wished upon the night
To see you, anew,
As my reflection rippled
And spoke of unbearable
Half-truths, of me and you
As I wiped my tearful eyes...

O.A.

Go Home to Your Wife

Go home to your wife
She said, I have nothing
For you here
I remember these words
Like it was a sign beware
It must have been
Divine intervention
Because I couldn't see
The honourable mention
I got for doing the right thing
When the ladies talked
Over the next few years
Go home to your wife
She said, you're better
Than this, my dear
My Dear.

I have nothing
For you here…
I remember these words
Like I had not been there…

O.A.

Authentic

Even at my worst time
When dark clouds
Have engulfed my halo
And the canteen
In which I collect donations
Has morosely dried up
From not enough love
Being handed out
To the streetside beguiled
Wanting to street perform
For an audience or crowd;
I hope the authenticity
Of my actions
And not my tears
Allows me to eleviate fears
Of the wisdom of the crowd.
By expressing words of vim
And vigour to stimulate life
And actions coming out
Of my fast talking mouth...

O.A.

Syntax of Your Heart

Sat up all night,
In my own Hackathon
With Mr. Mateo,
Deciphering not Java,
Ruby, or even Python
But rather the code,
Or linguistic nature,
Of the messages,
You sent me
In the letters,
I received on the day
You sailed far away
To the other side
Of the world:
To be a part
Of a new clique,
That would hack
The syntax of your heart
Better than I could or did
Before we ever fell apart...

P.S. I loved you
From the start.

O.A.

Part of the Arts

You cannot partake in the Arts
Without appreciating another Artist or two;
Or a thousand more who perform
Better than you;
If there so exists.
But you'll understand
The connection more and more
To your audience or afficionados,
If you open the doors to learning the score,
Of your favorite composer or violinist you adore,
In ways, then you appreciate what they do even more.

Song to the Moon.
Bell.

O.A.

What It Means to be An Artist

Imagination breeds,
Inconceivable needs,
That only a person who believes
In such, occupational dreams
Will overcome the desire to achieve
Such romanticized things, indeed.
An Artist is someone who bleeds
A discipline most fashionable to please
The emporium on the asthetic streets:
Like a filmmaker, novelist, sculptor, poet
Dancer, graphic artist, designer, in the humanities
But these days, an Artist can be just about anybody
With a will and way to pave their way
With a will and way to pave their way
With a will and way to pave their way
To the other side of tomorrow
To the other side of tomorrow

Originality indeed,
Offsets the bereaved,
That only a person who believes
In such, occupational dreams
Will overcome the desire to achieve
Such imaginative things, as they please.
An Artist is someone who dares to dream
And produce a piece of work akin, akin, akin
To all those creative people that came before her or him:
Like a producer, writer, entertainer, loop artist
Street performer, stage actor, singer, in the humanities
But these days, an Artist can be just about anybody
With a will and way to pave their way
With a will and way to pave their way
With a will and way to pave their way
To the other side of tomorrow
To the other side of tomorrow
And show how their Art can shine
And show how their Art can shine
And put a smile on the faces of those amused
Like a Star to a child

What it means to be an Artist
Is simply this...
The world is but a frequent kiss
From such people who choose
To showcase their love
As lightening in a bottle
For us, as an Artist
Creating in the image of God
Revealing their thoughts
And living in complete
Agony or blissfulness.

O.A.

On The Road to Pandemonium

I dream of the day
When I can salivate
At my table on stage
And sign my life away
Autograph by Autograph
To thousands of readers
Who have bought my books
And have given me sharp looks
In the streets, at all my favorite eats
Before I retreat, retreat, back to my home
And then cry, cry, cry tears of joy all alone.

I am on the road to Pandemonium
But I loathe the burden I carry on my own.
The world is unforgiving and I am now cold
The world is unforgiving and I am now cold
The world is unforgiving and I am now cold
The writer inside me yet warms my old soul
The writer inside me yet warms my old soul
The writer inside me yet warms my old soul
As I continue down this cobblestone road...
I am on the road to Pandemonium
But I loathe the burden I carry on my own.

I dream of the day
When I can salivate
At my table on stage
And sign my life away
Autograph by Autograph
To thousands of readers
Who have bought my books
Who originally had written me off
As a two-bit hack that couldn't cook
Anything up worth reading in any books
And didn't think I'd ever earn a second look.

I am on the road to Pandemonium
But I loathe the burden I carry on my own.
The world is unforgiving and I am now cold

The world is unforgiving and I am now cold
The writer inside me yet warms my old soul
The writer inside me yet warms my old soul
The writer inside me yet warms my old soul
As I continue down this cobblestone road...
I am on the road to Pandemonium
But I loathe the burden I carry on my own.

I am on the road to Pandemonium
But I loathe the burden I carry on my own...

O.A.

The Author Inside My Head

For Simply... Me.

The voice inside my head
Is not that of a Monster
The voice inside my head
Is that of a timid Author
Dying to be heard, or read
Whichever comes first
Before or after he is dead.
He stands on a podium
On my medulla oblongata
Between my two temples
And recites Cantatas:
Shakespeare, Hughes,
The Beats, Hemingway,
Donne, and Keats
Atwood, Plath,
And Maya Angelou
Among many others too.
He gives me ideas
In a brainstorm mood
And peers through my eyes
Like a fish in a glass pool
Bouncing from one window
To another Retina window
And back and forth through
My Occipital Lobes.
The Author knows,
When to steal the show
By giving me something
To say or write as he goes
Canvasing through
My sordid memory
For ideas to showcase
Out my glasses,
And down my nose.
Through my mouth
He'll shout: "Here's an idea!
Now write it down!!!!"

The voice inside my head
Is not that of a Monster
The voice inside my head
Is that of a timid Author
Dying to be heard, or read
Whichever comes first
Before or after he is dead.

He stands on a podium
On my medulla oblongata
Between my two temples
And recites Cantatas...

O.A.

If You Still Have Love For Me

I know it's hard
To accept these things
That I've put us through
But frankly, my dear
If you're still here
In the morning
I'll be greatful
I'll be fine

I want to watch the sun rise
With you by my side, one more time
I want to share a cup of coffee inside
I want to read the morning newspaper
I want to watch the morning news too
Anything with you

If you still have love for me
Then forgive me for my mistakes
Forgive me for not seeing the truth
Forgive me for not speaking of you
When I had the chance
This is my last waltz
My last dance
But if you still have love for me
Then believe, I still love you
I still love you

I know you trusted me
And I broke that trust
I've put you through Hell
But frankly, my dear
If you're still here
In the morning
I'll be greatful
I'll be fine

I want to watch the sun rise
With you by my side, one more time
I want to share a cup of coffee inside

I want to watch the morning news too
Anything with you

If you still have love for me
Then forgive me for my mistakes
Forgive me for not seeing the truth
Forgive me for not speaking of you
When I had the chance
This is my last waltz
My last dance
But if you still have love for me
Then believe, I still love you
I still love you

O.A.

For the World to be Alright

For the World to be Alright
You have to turn out the lights
On an ideal that's not right
At least that's what Theology
Explains...
Something has to die.

The burning cities
The flooding waters
The hurricanes
The rise of the insane
At least that's what Theology
Explains...
Something has to die.

For the World to be Alright
You have to put it out of sight
An ideal that's not so right
At least that's what Theology
Explains...
Something has to die.

The deserted feelings
The roof on the ceiling
The limitations
The vast imitations
At least that's what Theology
Explains...
Something has to die.

For the World to be Alright
You have to get this point right
You have to change your lives
Within you and me
At least that's what Theology
Explains...
Something has to die.

O.A.

What Giraffes Do

If the Lion, Tiger or Bear
Or any other animal
In the Animal Kingdom here
Needs a helping hand or two
A Giraffe will stick it's neck out
A Giraffe will wade in the pool
For you, as a lookout or help you
Through a tough spot
Through the thickest route
As a tall slender animal should.

But we don't appreciate the Giraffe
Like the Lions, Tigers and Bears do
But rather assume
They are getting in our business
Or are being rude.

In human life, are you like a Giraffe
Sticking it's neck out for other folks too
And feel under appreciated
When your words don't move them
As the way they do for you?

What Giraffes do
Is inexplicably cool.

O.A.

Fired Up!

We have won!
We have won!
    Let's take to the streets, pounding our drums, parumpa-pa-pom
    We got the Devil on the run, come everyone, come everyone.
    Let's join arms, with our beers, and our ostentatious cheers!
    And form a marching line, that will obliterate the dubious times
    And give birth, in a circle around this lamppost as a new sign
    For the greater things to come, in this world of ours that yearns
    For a greater light, to shine on the benign and people of concern.

We have won!
We have won!
    Come everyone, come everyone, listen to the heartbeat of the drums
    As we celebrate under the nighttime starlit god overlooking sky
    As the creator in this universe who dabbles with an all-seeing eye
    Let's join arms, with our beers, and our ostentatious cheers!
    And form a marching line, that will obliterate the dubious times
    And give birth, in a circle around this lamppost as a new sign
    As we celebrate the beginning of a new day, as we breath as one.

We have won!
We have won!
    A new day has arrived, right before our eyes, we'll stay up all night
    We'll stay up all night, through clouds of smoke, 'till sunrise.
    The celebration, and hard work has just begun, as we close our eyes
    And imagine a new world, without restrictions, and unlimited love.
    Let's join arms, with our beers, and our ostentatious cheers!
    And form a marching line, that will obliterate the dubious times
    And give birth, in a circle around this lamppost as a new sign.

We have won!
We have won!
    Come everyone, come everyone!
    Let the celebration begin, as we march for love.
We have won!
We have won!
    Let's march for unity, equality and things much higher.
    Let's march for all the times, we were under fire.
    Let's stand for all the things our ancestors could not.

We have won!
We have won!
    Come everyone, come everyone!
    Let the celebration begin, as we march for love.
    Let the celebration begin, as we march for love.
    Let the celebration begin, as we march for love.
    Let the celebration begin, as we march as one.

O.A.

The Lighthouse Paradigm

Inside every person
Inside every woman and man
There is a lighthouse
There is a light
Steering you away from all the negativity
Of the solemn day.

When the seas get rough
When a hurricane comes rollin' in
There is a lighthouse
There is a light
Steering you away from all the negativity
Of the solemn day.

In every crowd of people
There is keeper of the light
There is a person who is the lifeline
That connects every soul around
Like a lighthouse on the sea renowned
Signaling to passing boats to be safe and sound
And to avoid the negative persons who get you down.

Inside every person
Inside every woman and man
There is a lighthouse
There is a light
Steering you away from all the negativity
Of the solemn day.

The keeper of the light
The lighthouse inside your life
The light inside your light
Knows when a storm is coming
Knows when to let you get your boat running
Signaling to you now to be safe and sound
And to avoid the negative persons who get you down.

Inside every person
Inside every woman and man
There is a lighthouse

There is a light
Steering you away from all the negativity
Of the solemn day.

O.A.

The Mosquito & the Spider

In my mind, my fruitful mind
There is a time for innovation
And concentration
And then there is a time
For innocence and meditation
But when thoughts get jumbled up
When things misfire out of turn
A Spider appears to spin a web
Of deceitful yearn.

In my mind, my fruitful mind
There is a time for information
And exacerbation
And then there is a time
For experimentation and regulation
But when thoughts are ripe
With ideas that can change your life
A Mosquito appears in the web
Of deceitful yearn.

Idle thoughts are not nice
Especially when the Mosquito
Of thought infects you twice
It can only struggle to get out
Against a web of deceitful lies
When I tell myself the Mosquito
Yearns for more light.

It's a pity that this thought bites
Or stings, but then that's the thing!
Will you slap your head
To make dead the fruitful thought
That's caught in a Spider's web?
Trying to kill the Mosquito of light
Who has infected your heart/mind
Like an idea that wants out, to fly?

I only ask you this
Because my mind won't listen

But then, that's the beauty of a lightbulb
Shining directly on the cavern of the mind
Showing the symptomatic signs
Of what happens when a great idea in life
Does not get enough support to shine...

O.A.

Mothers are Special

When a boy or girl enters this vast world
It's through a woman whose love unfurls
In a time when love bears a fruitful labour
To deliver a baby upon the medical table.
The Doctors and Nurses or Midwives know
That through the years the bond will grow;
And that first sign of a baby look into eyes
Shows that there is more to this surprise,
There's a bond of a Mother and a new life.

If the Father is present, he can show care
But a Father can be replaced if he is not there
But for a woman who knows the baby stuff
It's a hard road ahead for a baby to grow up.
For each Mother that bears a child or two,
The world is a playground for their child too;
And if that child at 21, 33, or 42 crosses lines
That Mother can teach them wrong from right;
As she brought he or she into this world of light,
Because it's through her, heaven was sent best
And a Mother's fears, will never be laid to rest.

So Mothers are special all the way around
Anywhere in the world a Mother is profound
And do not think a Mother will not fight the fight
To make sure their child grows up with rights;
Because a Mother is a walking angel of love
In each child's angelic, precious life from God.

O.A.

In Memory of The Fallen

A Remembrance Day Poem.

In memory of the fallen
The men and women
Who served this country well
Let us bow our heads
And remember those soldiers who bled.
The price of freedom is never cheap
As I stand here before the graves that weep
For our fallen soldiers that lay beneath
Lest we forget, their memories are ours to keep.
A country is made up of men and women
Who swear allegiance to the Crown
To defend and honour that sovereignty
And all the children from each town.

In memory of the fallen
The men and women
Who served this country well
Let us bow our heads
And remember those soldiers who bled.
Let us say a prayer to cross the universe
To wish our departed in heaven
And hope where they are now
There are poppies growing for our brethren.
In Remembrance for the battles won
The price of freedom is never cheap
For the people who fight for: "Freedom, Peace and Love,"
May their souls, soar high above, and be reached.

In memory of the fallen
The men and women
Who served this country well
Let us bow our heads
And remember those soldiers who bled.
Let us say a prayer or two today
For our commrades, family members, and friends
Who served, and still serve our country to the end.

My Personal Lawyer

I've known him for years
And he's seen me go through it all
From being a junkie on the streets
To waiting tables at all my favorite eats
The man has stood by me,
And I don't really know why?
Other than he likes to see me surprised.
But if the day comes along,
When he can no longer carry on,
Supporting the train wreck I've become
I'll stop to let him off and thank the boss
For not shooting this self-loathing Albatross.

My personal lawyer may not call me up
To counterfeit the moon,
But I know if I need to talk to someone
He'll offer me a seat in his platoon.
May God bless the dude,
For putting up with me,
All these last few years too.

O.A.

Air Hugs

Salutations my Dear!!!
It's been quite the year
Covid-19 has changed,
Changed many brains,
As to how, we think
About greeting others
When we're out and about.
But one thing is for sure
As the world turns more
And as the elbow bump
Becomes the silent norm
"Air hugs" will become
The thing to do alot more
When we meet at the mall
Or at the grocery store...
Or just when we're bored
And don't want to touch
Anybody around us anymore.

O.A.

Sometimes, You Just Need to Cry

Sometimes, you just need to cry
Sometimes, for no reason at all in your life
Sometimes, the stress is so great
Sometimes, it's the only way people can relate

Sometimes, you just need to cry
Sometimes, it's when you've lost someone in life
Sometimes, the money has run dry
Sometimes, it's when someone in your life has died

For whatever reason
For whatever circumstance
You may need to shed a tear or two
You may need to do this, to get back to you

Sometimes, you just need to cry
Sometimes, for no reason at all in your life
Sometimes, the stress is so great
Sometimes, it's the only way people can relate

Sometimes,
You just need to cry
You just need to cry
Sometimes,
You just need to close your eyes
And let all your emotions subside.

O.A.

In the Spirit of Christmas

On Christmas Eve,
When I saw a child weep
For the toy he wanted
From a store
That didn't carry it anymore,
I drove across town
To bring his parents
One that I found around
From off the sales floor...

The child was elated,
His parents were elevated
And I thought I had done
My one, Christmas deed
To make everyone
Happy this Christmas Eve...

So it is with the holidays
These days anyways,
People seldom
Look to help anyone
Walking their way...

But in the Spirit of Christmas
The world could use
Some holiday cheer
Each and every year
Like this child,
Who almost shed tears
About the toy
They did not have here.

See Chistmas
Is about giving
Celebrating and giving
Much more than
Just lending an ear...

So in the Spirit of Christmas
For the holidays

This year and every year
I hope you remember
To give and celebrate
Our Lord Jesus Christ's
Birthday...

By spreading some holiday
Cheers...

O.A.

I Do Not Care

I do not care
I do not care if you dislike me
I do not care about the autumn wind
Blowing in my uncut hair
Nor the leaves blown about the trashy lawn
As I get up to go to work, excuse me while I yawn!!!
I do not care, I do not care, I do not care.

I do not care
I do not care if you do not want me here
I do not care if you think I should die
A most horrible Death
Nor do I care about what you say under your breath
As I get up to get a cup of coffee in the office at work
I do not care, I do not care, I do not care.

Because you may want to see me cry
Or die, a horrible Death a thousand times
But I have bad news for almost all of you
I have bills and expenses like you do too
And well you like money?
Well honey, like my mother would always say...
Well I like my money too.

O.A.

The Angel On Top of Our Christmas Tree

For Alice

One Christmas Eve
One night in my memory
My parents were arguing
About something I couldn't believe
When my sister said to me:
"Do you believe in miracles?
Do you believe in angels, lately?"

I said to her wide-eyed
As a little boy would
"I believe in Santa Claus"
And then I asked:
"How bout you?"

My sister answered
In a strong tone,
"Look up at our Christmas Tree
There is an angel
In our home, we're not alone!!!"

I said to her wide-eyed
As a little boy would,
"How do you know it's real?"
And then I asked:
"Do you think it can see us?"

My sister answered
Once again in a strong tone
"It's lighting up brighter and bright
There is an angel
In our home, we're gonna be alright!!!"

My parents stopped arguing
As soon as the angel got bright
My sister and I
Came out from under the couch
And begged them to stop fighting
Tonight

My father wept
My mother wept
And we all stood there
Confused and perplexed.

Then my sister answered
Once again in a strong tone
"Thank you dear angel for the light
Thank you dear angel for saving our lives
And for being in our home, on this night..."

And then my father looked up
And said: "We have been rude
Happy Birthday to you
My Saviour Lord Jesus Christ
Merry Christmas to you
And thank you angel
For saving our lives...
Forgive me
For arguing with my wife..."

The angel dimmed
And a sound like a choir outside
Begun to sing gospel hymns
And my father said to us all
"Christmas is about love,
Respect and giving back
So let's be merry afterall
And let's have a good night..."

O.A.

The Eden Restoration Project

I.
Life is precious
Life is right
Life on this planet is courageously bright
We deserve clean air each and every night
We deserve to treat Mother Nature as right
There is no more garden of Eden around
Unless we restore our forests, and stop them
From burning down, to the forsaken ground
Let's restore the globe to the state it was
Like it was a new gift from our heavenly God.

The Eden Restoration Project
The foundation of new creation
The movement to restore the planet
Is now in the hands of those who can handle it
The next generation can help with restoration
The next generation can help with emancipation
But today's generation has to help with amalgamation.

Climate change is changing the world
Changing our ocean life for the worse
Turning our clear blue skies into night
Turning clean air into pollution sights
Of smog-filled smokestacks on sites.
Our forests are burning at a rapid rate
Our Amazon Rain Forest is dying too
Our farmers deal with topsoil erosion
While livestock are still slaughtered
When investors have nothing to lose.

The Eden Restoration Project
The foundation of new creation
The movement to restore the planet
Is now in the hands of those who can handle it
The next generation can help with restoration
The next generation can help with emancipation
But today's generation has to help with amalgamation.

Climate change is changing our world
Changing life for every boy and girl
Turning garbage landfills into hot spots
Turning recycling into a way of cleaning lots
Of mounds of garbage left out to dry.
Our way of life is changing around us too
Our groceries are being used up through
Our farmers are doing all they can to help
While we devour what's on the store shelves
When people do nothing to help themselves.

The Eden Restoration Project
The foundation of new creation
The movement to restore the planet
Is now in the hands of those who can handle it
The next generation can help with restoration
The next generation can help with emancipation
But today's generation has to help with amalgamation.

So, I urge you to look to the news
Check your sources, follow through
Look at the person in the mirror too
See if there's anything you can do
To slow the course we're abiding to.

Life is precious
Life is right
Life on this planet is courageously bright
We deserve clean air each and every night
We deserve to treat Mother Nature as right
There is no more garden of Eden around
Unless we restore our forests, and stop them
From burning down, to the forsaken ground
Let's restore the globe to the state it was
Like it was a new gift from our heavenly God.

Still, I urge you to look to the news
Check your sources, follow through
Look at the person in the mirror too
See if there's anything you can do
To slow the course we're abiding to.

Let's restore the globe to the state it was
Like it was a new gift from our heavenly God.
Life is precious
Life is right
Life on this planet
Is courageously bright
There is no more garden of Eden around
But with enough love we can restore the world
To what God originally intended for it to abound.

O.A.

Christmas Morning

It's Christmas Morning
Here in our house,
And everyone is still asleep
And tired from going out,
The night before, of course
In attending midnight Church Mass.
We sang our hearts out
The Christmas hymns of the past,
But now all is quiet
All has calmed down,
From the night before
From all our guests in the house.
Now we'll thank our parents
For giving Santa our lists
And count our blessings
That we were not missed!!!
All before we drink egg nog
And eat cookies once more
And celebrate Christmas
By stepping out the front door
Into a winter wonderland
Where we build Snowmen
And have snowball fights.

It's Christmas Morning
Here in our house,
And everyone is still asleep
And tired from going out,
The night before, of course
But us kids know too well
How to wake everyone up,
By jumping on the beds
And bringing tea cups,
To our sleepy parents
Who do not want to get up.

It's Christmas Morning
Here in our house,
And everyone is still asleep
And tired from going out,

The night before, of course
But everyone knows too well
In the end it's a celebration
Around the neighbourhood
Around the world
Getting together,
Again and again,
Enjoying each other
And opening presents
With family, and friends.

O.A.

Eureka! Eureka!

The Covid -19 mask you wear
Hides your face and hair
But when you remove it
And let us see you there
It's a whole new you
Behind the facade
Of artificial flair...
The joy of
Discovering
A whole new you
Brings waterducts
Of joy to a whole
New product.
Like a Yukon
Golden nugget
I didn't know
You were
Smiling
Behind
There.

O.A.

The Boy is Hardly a Man

If he cannot stand the heat
In the kitchen
And if there's something
You think he's missin'
The boy might hardly be a man
The boy might hardly be a man.
Of mice and men
The journey ends
Turning this boy
Into a righteous man
The world understands
As the hands become calloused
The boy might hardly be a man
The boy might hardly be a man.
All in a day's work
All to feed his family
To render himself to life
On the plate of civil obedience
Might put the desire in his eyes
To be more than just a wise guy
The boy might hardly be a man
The boy might hardly be a man.
But the world understands
As the hands become calloused
A young man is born
A man within a man is torn
To become a king within his lands
To face his fears, and to kill the beast
With his bare knuckled hands
The boy might one day be a man
The boy might one day be a man.
There is hope
At the end of the rope
That one day
The boy who stands
Firm in his command
Will one day become a man.

O.A.

A Rodeo Clown and His Dancing Shoes

In hopes of maintaining a close relationship
With you, my tangible Muse
I will jump through the fire
I will vault the stratosphere
I will leap over the sword-shaped moon
I will leap much, much higher
I will walk across a highwire
Just to support you
As you would do for me too
As you would love me too.

In hopes of winning you over
To my side, my side of the war
I will fight to have you near
I will calm your growing fears
I will warm your heart here
I will do what I need to do
I will be there just for you
Just to support you
As you would do for me too
As you would love me too.

Just to support you
There's nothing I would not do
To make you laugh,
I would act a fool,
I would be your Clown
If you would be my Muse.

I would be your Rodeo Clown
If you would be my dancing shoes
Together, there's nothing
We could not do...

Together, we could face the bull
And then dance our way
To the moon.

O.A.

Music

By

Oliver Allen

2021

Love You Like a Violin

Beautiful Sunset

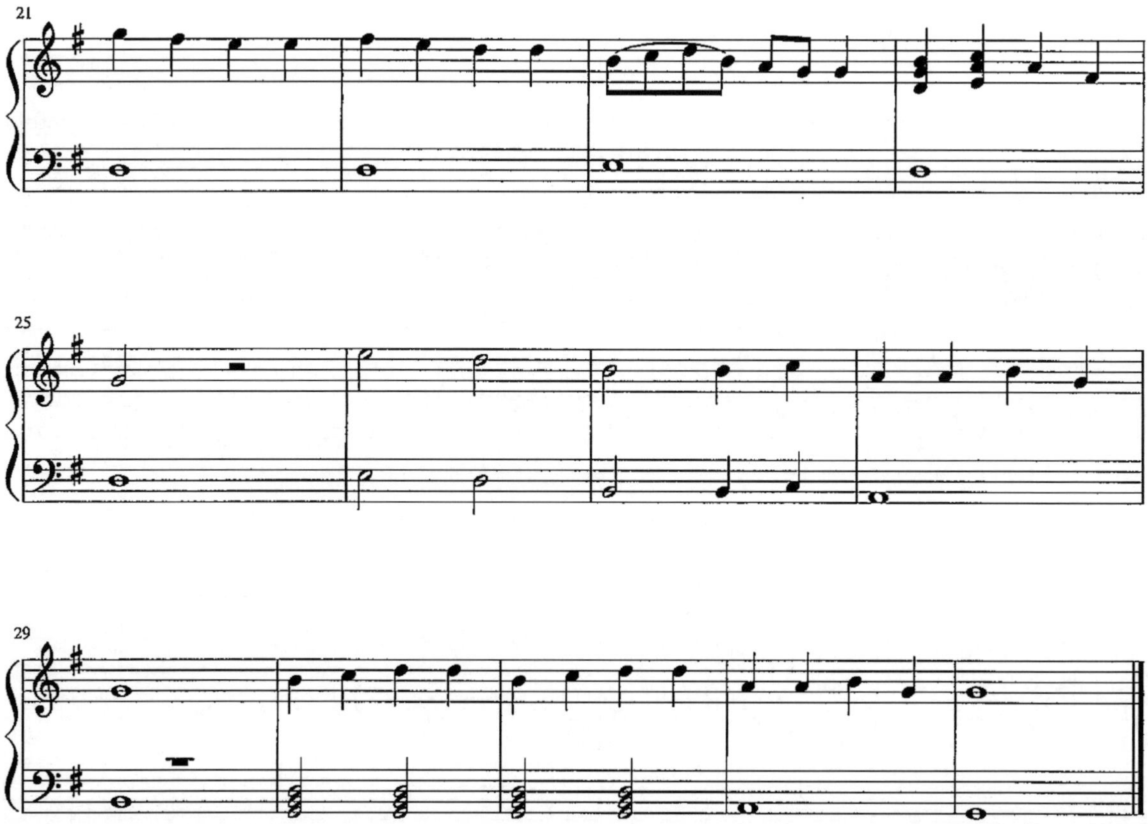
21
25
29

Exquisitely Yours

A Postcard From Vancouver

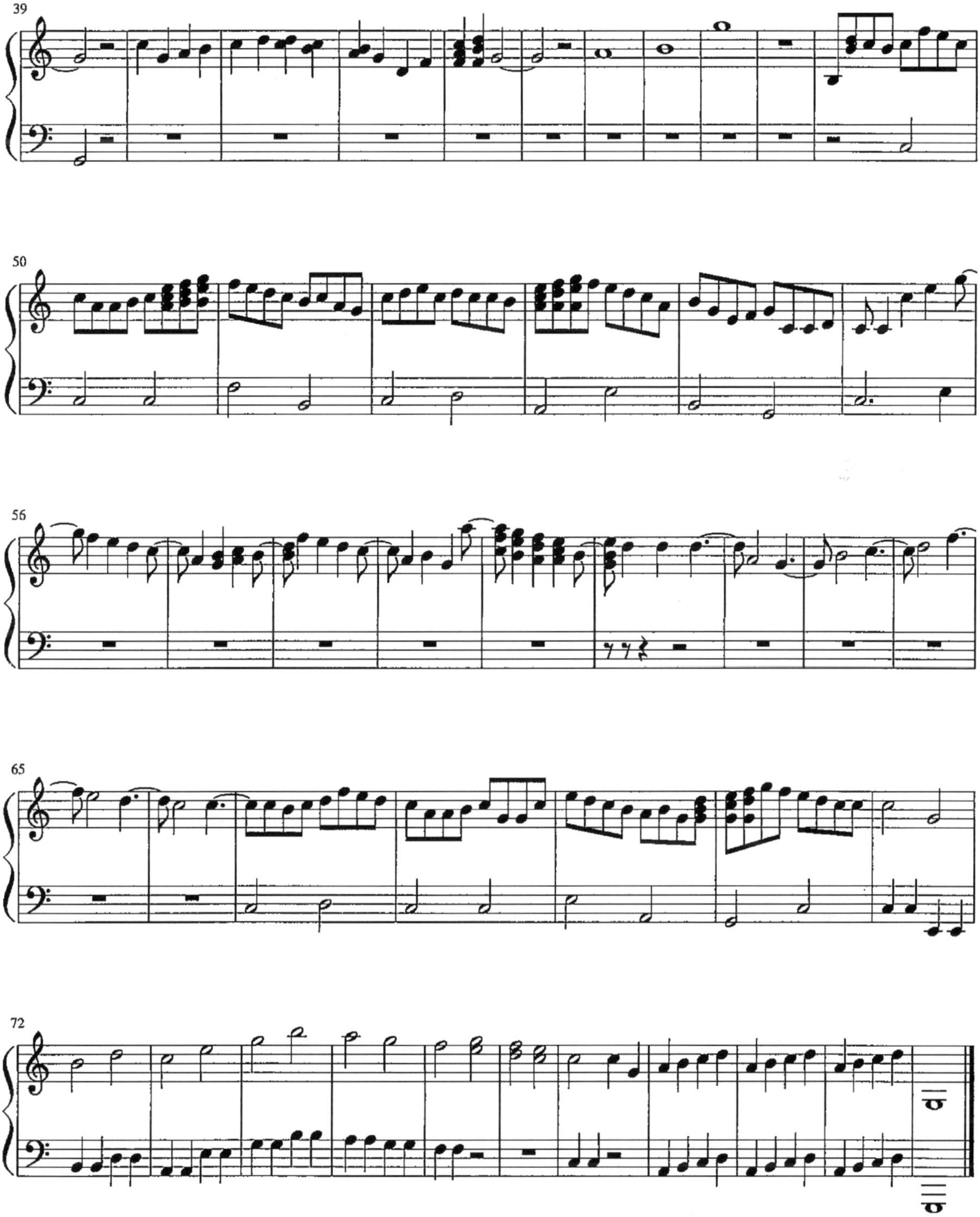
39
50
56
65
72

A Small Man Among Giants

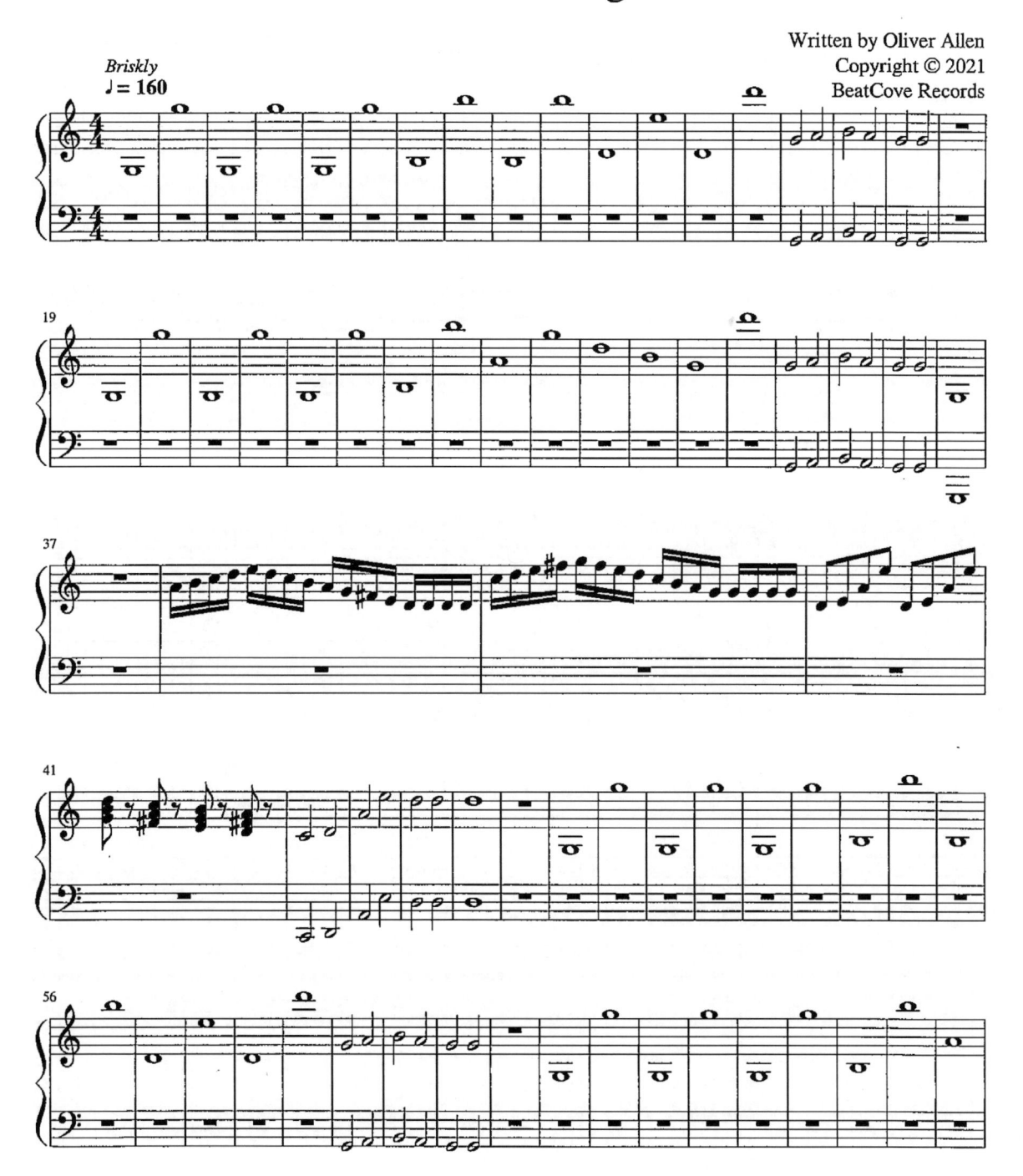

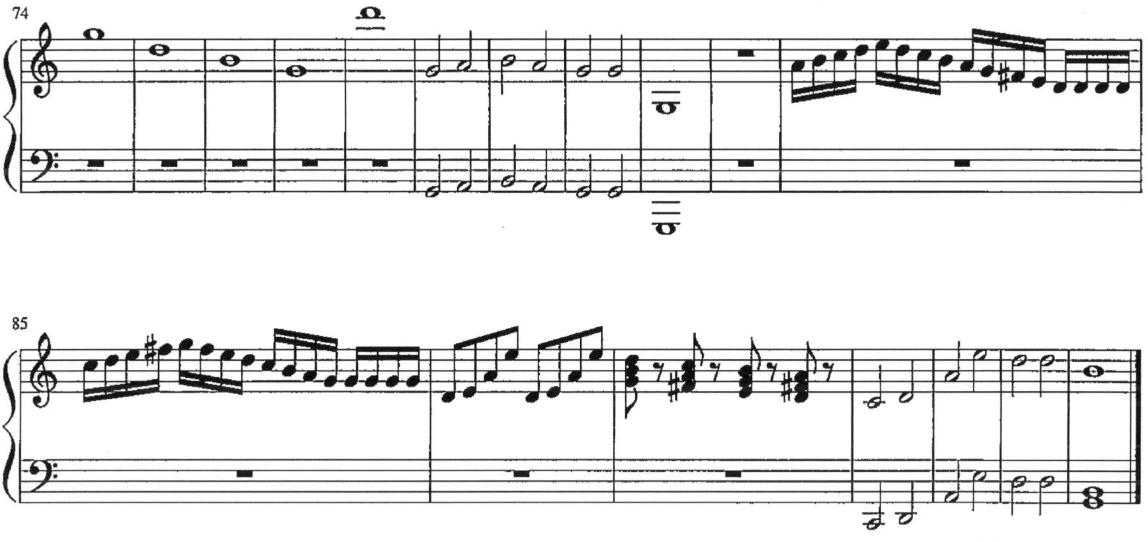
74
85

WARRIOR
A Song Cycle for Quartet

Written by Oliver Allen
Copyright © 2021
BeatCove Records

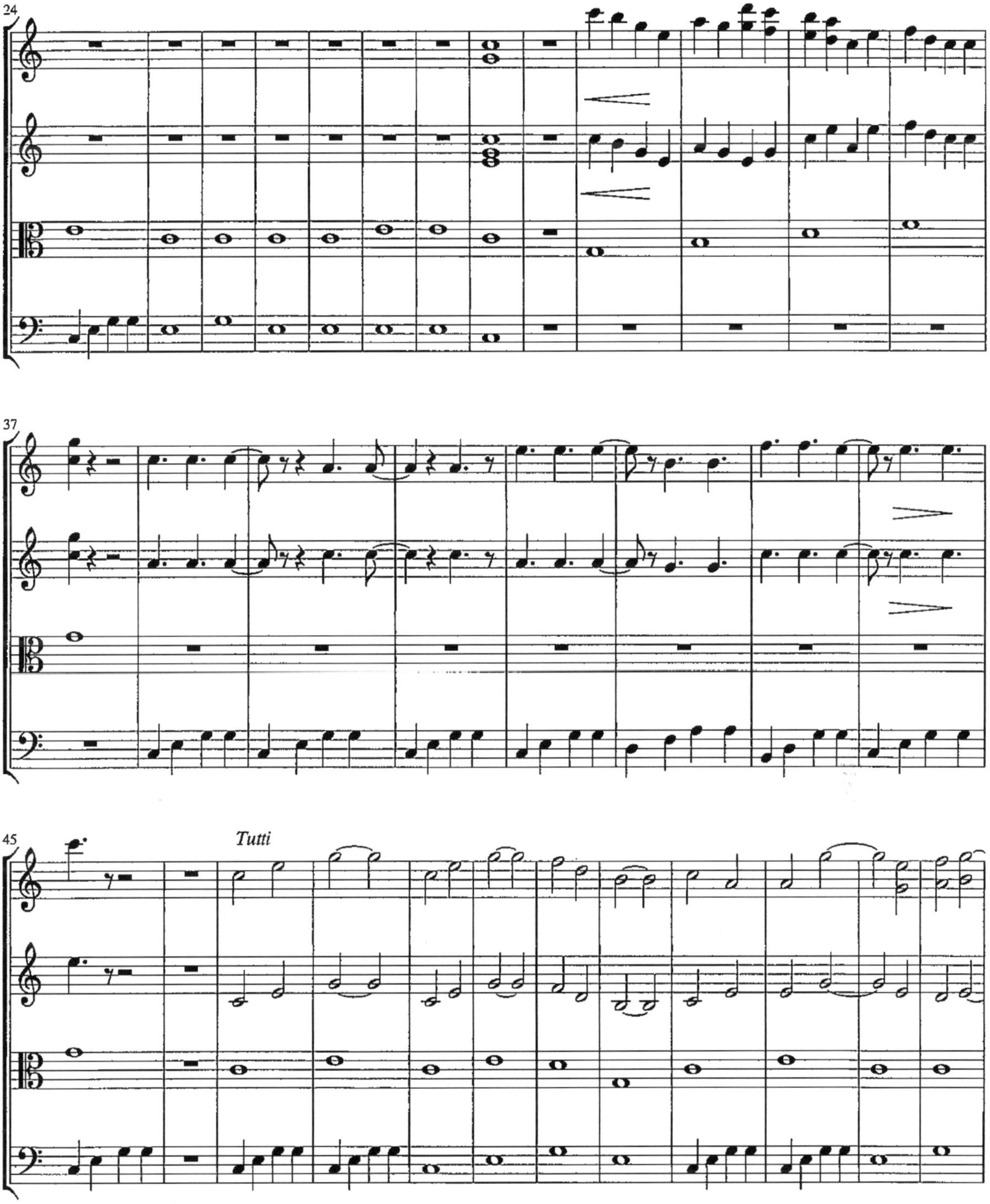
24
37
45
Tutti

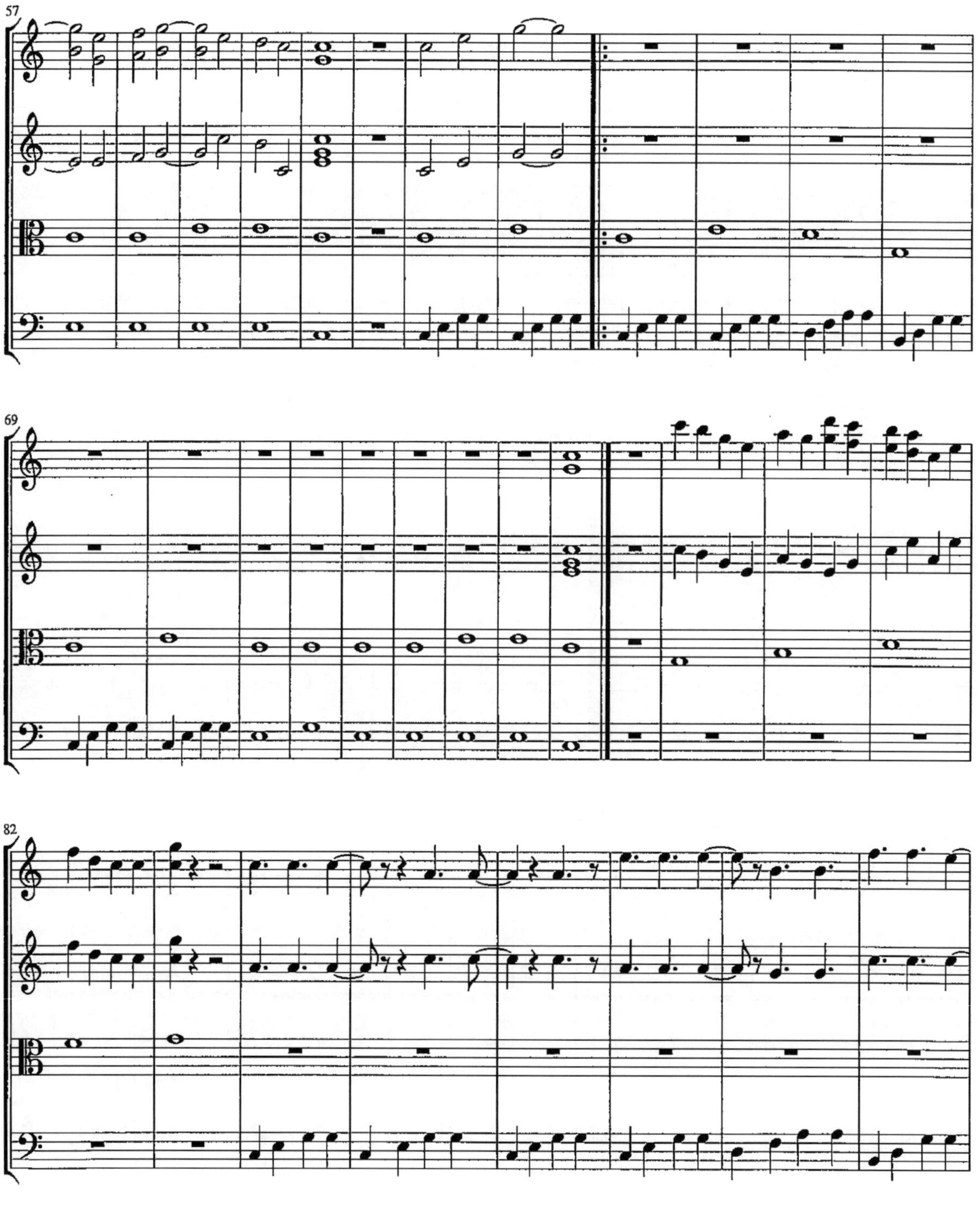
57
69
82

ONYX

Written by Oliver Allen
Copyright © 2021
BeatCove Records

Lively with Feeling
♩ = 100

Granville Island Blues

Written by Oliver Allen
Copyright © 2021
BeatCove Records

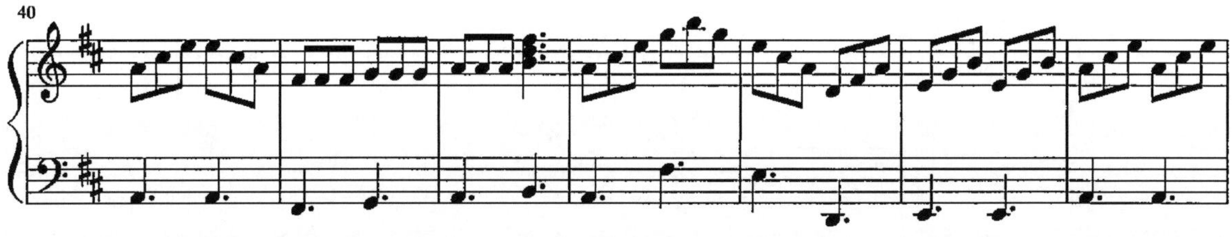
40

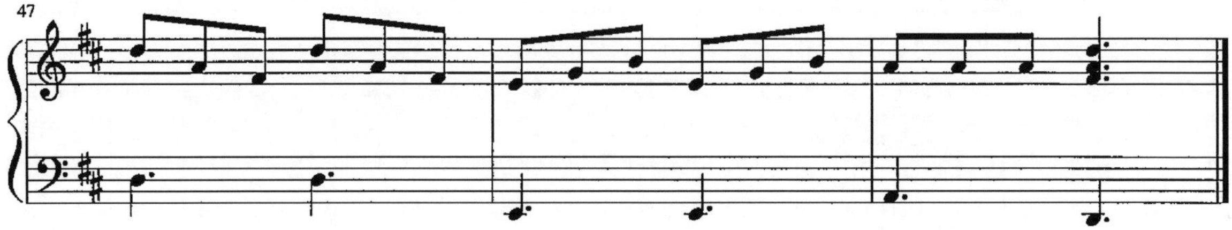
47

Manufactured by Amazon.ca
Bolton, ON